Praise
And Worship

by A.L. and Joyce Gill

ISBN 0-941975-33-9
© Copyright 1988,1995

*It is illegal and a violation of Christian ethics
to reproduce any part of this manual
without the written permission of the authors.*

*Powerhouse Publishing
P.O. Box 99
Fawnskin, CA 92333
(909) 866-3119*

Books by A.L. and Joyce Gill

God's Promises for Your Every Need

Destined for Dominion

Out! In the Name of Jesus

Victory over Deception!

Manuals in This Series

Authority of the Believer
*How to Quit Losing
And Start Winning*

God's Provision for Healing
*Receiving and Ministering
God's Healing Power*

Ministry Gifts
*Apostle, Prophet, Evangelist,
Pastor, Teacher*

Miracle Evangelism
God's Plan to Reach the World

New Creation Image
Knowing Who You Are in Christ

Patterns for Living
From the Old Testament

Praise and Worship
Becoming Worshipers of God

Supernatural Living
*Through the Gifts of the
Holy Spirit*

About the Authors

A.L. and Joyce Gill are internationally known speakers, authors and Bible teachers. A.L.'s apostolic ministry travels have taken him to over fifty nations of the world, preaching in person to crowds exceeding one hundred thousand and to many millions by radio and television.

Their top-selling books and manuals have sold over two million copies in the United States. Their writings, which have been translated into many languages, are being used in Bible schools and seminars around the world.

The powerful life-changing truths of God's Word explode in the lives of others through their dynamic preaching, teaching, writing and video and audio tape ministry.

The awesome glory of the presence of God is experienced in their praise and worship seminars as believers discover how to become true and intimate worshipers of God. Many have discovered a new and exciting dimension of victory and boldness through their teachings on the authority of the believer.

The Gills have trained many believers to step into their own God-given supernatural ministries with the healing power of God flowing through their hands. Many have learned to be supernaturally natural as they are released to operate in all nine gifts of the Holy Spirit in their daily lives and ministries.

Both A.L. and Joyce have Master of Theological Studies degrees. A.L. has also earned a Doctor of Philosophy in Theology degree from Vision Christian University. Their ministry is solidly based on the Word of God, is centered on Jesus, strong in faith and taught in the power of the Holy Spirit.

Their ministry is a demonstration of the Father's heart of love. Their preaching and teaching are accompanied by powerful anointing, signs, wonders, and healing miracles with many being slain in waves under the power of God.

Signs of revival including waves of holy laughter, weeping before the Lord and awesome manifestations of God's glory and power are being experienced by many who attend their meetings.

A Word to Teachers and Students

In the study of **Praise and Worship**, believers will discover the joy of moving into God's presence and releasing their spirits in all of the powerful, fresh, biblical expressions of high praise and intimate worship to God. By the truths revealed in this book, believers will become daily worshipers of God.

Powerful breakthroughs in the Spirit will occur in the lives of all who will "press into God" with a new determination to release their body, soul and spirit to experience all that is revealed in these powerful, life-changing studies.

It is important that time is spent in not only studying these truths, but also in practicing and experiencing all that is revealed in these lessons. As this happens, the overwhelming presence and glory of God will be manifested.

We suggest that before teaching this course you read the books and listen to the tapes that are listed as **Suggested Reading and Listening.** The more you saturate yourself with the truths of God's Word concerning praise and worship, the more these truths will move from your mind into your spirit. This manual will then provide the outline for you to use as you impart these truths to others.

Personal life illustrations are a must for effective teaching. The author has omitted these from this work so that the teacher will provide illustrations from his or her own rich experiences, or those of others to which the students will be able to relate. It should always be remembered that it is the Holy Spirit who has come to teach us all things, and that when we are studying or when we are teaching we should always be empowered and led by the Holy Spirit.

This study is excellent for personal or group studies, Bible schools, Sunday schools and home groups.

It is important that both the teacher and the student have copies of this manual during the course of the study. The best books are written in, underlined, meditated on and digested. We have left space for your notes and comments. The format has been designed with a fast reference system for review and to assist you in finding areas again. This special format makes it possible for each person, once they have studied through this material, to teach the contents to others. Paul wrote to Timothy:

> **And the things that you have heard from me among many witnesses, commit these to faithful men who will be able to teach others also. 2 Timothy 2:2b**

This manual is designed for multiplication in the lives, the ministry and the future teaching of others. We believe it is God's plan for each student to become a teacher.

Table of Contents

*Scriptures in **Praise And Worship***
*are taken from the **New King James Version.***
Copyright 1979, 1980, 1982 by Thomas Nelson Inc., Publishers.

Suggested Reading and Listening

The Tabernacle Of David
By Kevin J. Conner – Bible Temple Publishing
7545 N.E. Glisan Street, Portland, Oregon 97213, U.S.A.

The Power Of Praise And Worship
By Terry Law – Victory House, Inc.
P.O. Box 700238, Tulsa, Oklahoma 94170, U.S.A.

Hosanna Praise Tapes
Integrity Music, Inc.
P.O. Box 16813, Mobile, Alabama 36616 U.S.A

Acknowledgment
It is with great appreciation that we acknowledge
the contribution of Lin Rang for her many hours of work on this
manual. Her suggestions and additions have
contributed greatly to it's completion.

Introduction

Even as the Aaronic priests entered daily into the Tabernacle of Moses and later into Solomon's Temple, today we as believer-priests are to come daily into His Presence.

The Tabernacle of Moses consisted of gates which led into the courts. All believers could come into the courts. The priests moved through the courts to minister to the Lord in the Holy Place. Once a year, the High Priest entered into the Holy of Holies which contained the Ark of the Covenant.

The Holy of Holies was the earthly counterpart of the heavenly throne room of God. The Ark, which was covered with the Mercy Seat was the earthly place, the type of the throne of God. To be in the Holy of Holies was to be in the very Presence of God.

At the moment Jesus died on the cross, the veil which separated man from God was supernaturally torn from top to bottom. Man no longer needed to be separated from God because of sin. Man's sins could be forgiven. Now, men and women could boldly enter into God's Presence.

Even as there was a progression of entering in by the Old Testament priests, there is a progression of entering in today, as we as believer-priests come daily into His Presence in praise and worship. We are to enter in daily in our own private time of praise. We are to enter in corporately, with the whole body, whenever we assemble together. To enter requires an act of obedience on our part. God desires that we enter into His Presence, but we must take the initiative to do so.

First we are instructed by David to:

Enter into His gates with thanksgiving, And into His courts with praise. Be thankful to Him, and bless His name. Psalm 100:4.

We enter His gates with thanksgiving. We cannot enter His gates with ungrateful hearts. Our first songs as we are entering into praise should be ones that express our heartfelt thanksgiving unto the Lord.

As we come through the gates, we are in the courtyard. There must be a progression of entering into His Presence. We are not ready to go charging into the Holy of Holies in the most intimate time of awesome worship, until we have first spent time in the courtyard. In the courts we are instructed to praise. Here we joyfully enter into singing, music, clapping and raising our hands and, oftentimes, in dancing before the Lord as we express our praise.

As we linger in the courts of praise, we begin to feel a drawing within our spirits to come closer to God. Slowly, we are overcome by who He is. We begin to enter into a higher form of praise. We enter into the inner courts, into the Holy Place in worship.

Suddenly, we are no longer dancing or clapping our hands. We become so aware of the Presence of God that our hands begin to raise to Him in awesome reverence. The music has slowed. What was in order a moment before has suddenly stopped. The holiness of God's Presence is almost overwhelming.

As we continue to press in tears may be flowing down our cheeks. Sometimes all that we can do is stop playing and singing and remain silent in His Holy Presence. We are unaware of those around us. We are totally aware of God. We are standing in His Presence, lost in His love.

Almost without realizing it we have slipped, even as the High Priests, within the veil. We are standing in the Holy of Holies. We are in the close, intimate Presence of God. The anointing and power is beyond description. Many will bow or prostrate themselves before Him. Some may be slain in the Spirit.

We have a beautiful description of the time when the Ark of the Covenant was brought into Solomon's Temple,

And it came to pass, when the priests came out of the holy place, that the cloud filled the house of the LORD, so that the priests could not continue ministering because of the cloud; for the glory of the LORD filled the house of the LORD. 1 Kings 8:10,11

Today, too few believers have experienced this. We should prepare our hearts. We enter according to His instructions and pattern. We release our spirits, our souls and our bodies into a free and prolonged expression of unrestricted praise while we are in the courts.

We should continue to draw closer to God. He desires to be intimate with His bride. But, we must press in, closer and closer, until we are totally at one with Him. How God desires these moments of intimacy with each one. Our hearts must be set, committed and continually long for these precious, holy, indescribable moments of true worship.

Once we have entered in, we must not shrink back from His Presence. We must hold on and linger. As we do our lives will be changed. We are held so close, that an indelible impression of His character is made upon our spirits. The more time we spend totally in His Presence, totally intimate with Him, the more our spirits are conformed to His image, the more our lives will be changed into the image of His Son Jesus, the more we will become like Him.

It is here that there is the highest level of communion. It is here that we can clearly hear from Him. Our heart cry should agree with that of David when he wrote:

As the deer pants for the water brooks, so pants my soul for You, O God. My soul thirsts for God, for the living God. When shall I come and appear before God? Psalms 42:1,2

It was King David who brought the Ark back to Jerusalem after it had been captured. David was a man who had a heart after God and who sought continually after His Presence. For forty years, until the Temple of Solomon was built, the Ark, representing the Presence of God, dwelt in the Tabernacle of David. There was no veil which separated man from God. The Ark was in full view of all the worshipers. The only sacrifices in the Tabernacle of David were the continued sacrifices of praise to God. The Tabernacle of David has become the pattern of worship for the Church today.

James quoted Amos 9:11,12 when he wrote:

"On that day I will raise up the tabernacle of David, which has fallen down, and repair its damages; I will raise up its ruins, and rebuild it as in the days of old; that they may possess the remnant of Edom, and all the Gentiles who are called by My name," says the LORD who does this thing.

Today, we are experiencing the fulfillment of these prophecies as God is restoring true praise and worship to His Church. Like David, let each of us desire streams of living water during these times of refreshing. Let us move into His Presence and release our spirits in fresh, new and powerful expressions of praise to God.

My prayer is that you will be drawn closer and closer into the Presence of God and experience the intimacy and the life-changing experience of true worship.

Lesson One

Praise and Worship

Introduction

There is a fresh, new move of the Holy Spirit being experienced around the world. Once the worship services in many churches were dry and mournful. Traditional songs were half-heartedly sung from musty old hymn books. Today, it would not be unusual to find believers in many churches standing, singing, clapping their hands and even dancing in praise before the Lord. Many are experiencing the meaning of true worship as they kneel with hands raised to God, with tears streaming down their faces, lost in the Presence of God as they sing songs of intense worship to Him.

Instruments of all types are returning to the church. The congregation is no longer being entertained by choirs, or vocalists, who have little relationship themselves with God. Instead, the believers are experiencing the anointing of God in a fresh new way.

Often the glory of God fills the auditorium as His power sweeps across the congregation in wave after wave. As in the days of the dedication of the Temple, it is impossible to stand because of the cloud of His glory.

1 Kings 8:10,11 And it came to pass, when the priests came out of the holy place, that the cloud filled the house of the LORD, so that the priests could not continue ministering because of the cloud; for the glory of the LORD filled the house of the Lord.

David's Exhortation

David was a man who knew how to give praise to God. Let his words of exhortation draw us into the middle of what the Holy Spirit is doing today in the restoration of true worship to His Church.

Psalms 150:1-6 Praise the LORD! Praise God in His sanctuary; praise Him in His mighty firmament! Praise Him for His mighty acts; praise Him according to His excellent greatness! Praise Him with the sound of the trumpet; praise Him with the lute and harp! Praise Him with the timbrel and dance; praise Him with stringed instruments and flutes! Praise Him with loud cymbals; praise Him with high sounding cymbals! Let everything that has breath praise the LORD. Praise the LORD!

We should praise the Lord!

Definitions

➢ *Praise*

Praise is an expression of heartfelt gratitude and thanksgiving to God for all that He has done for us. It is a physical and vocal expression of our sincere appreciation to God for all of the wonderful blessings He has provided.

➢ *Worship*

Worship is the highest form of praise. Going beyond the thoughts of all of His wonderful blessings to us, we are expressing our admiration and commending God Himself for His person, character, attributes and perfection.

We are ministering to God for who He is and not just for what He has done for us.

PRAISE AND WORSHIP COMPARED

Praise

Praise is:

➢ *To speak well of*

➢ *To express admiration for*

➢ *To compliment*

➢ *To commend*

➢ *To congratulate*

➢ *To applaud*

➢ *To eulogize*

➢ *To extol*

Praise is talking, or singing, about God – how wonderful He is, what He has done for us.

Worship

Worship is:

➢ *To express reverence*

➢ *To have a sense of awe*

➢ *To bow low before the object of worship*

➢ *To esteem the worth of*

➢ *To give place to*

Worship is talking, or singing to God. You have passed the point of thinking about the things He has done and entered into worship of Him for who He is.

➤ *The Highest Praise*

Worship is the highest form of praise.

First it is:

➤ *An attitude of the heart*

➤ *A reverent occupation with the Creator*

➤ *A beginning of inner musings of the heart*

➤ *A depth of meditation upon the greatness and worthiness of God*

Then it is a spontaneous overflow of these thoughts and emotions. Worship cannot be "worked up," it must be entered into.

Finally, it is the outpouring of the soul in deep expressions of reverence, awe, wonder and adoration.

WHAT IS WORSHIP?

Before we can enter into worship, it is necessary to understand what worship is.

In Spirit

We can only give true worship to God from our spirits.

John 4:24 God is Spirit, and those who worship Him must worship in spirit and truth.

To worship in spirit is to worship with our whole heart. To worship in spirit also means to worship from our spirits by the power of the Holy Spirit, all of which reside in the same inner most place which the Bible calls our heart, or spirit.

In Truth

To worship in truth is to worship and allow the Lord to search the inner depths of our heart.

Proverbs 20:27 The spirit of a man is the lamp of the LORD, searching all the inner depths of his heart.

John 14:16,17 And I will pray the Father, and He will give you another Helper, that He may abide with you forever, even the Spirit of truth, whom the world cannot receive, because it neither sees Him nor knows Him; but you know Him, for He dwells with you and will be in you.

Cleanse Ourselves

Since we cannot worship God in the flesh it is important to cleanse ourselves of all fleshly thoughts and evil so that our spirits can worship God by His Spirit.

Colossians 3:5 Therefore put to death your members which are on the earth: fornication, uncleanness, passion, evil desire, and covetousness, which is idolatry.

Colossians 3:16,17 Let the word of Christ dwell in you richly in all wisdom, teaching and admonishing one another in psalms and hymns and spiritual songs, singing with grace in your hearts to the Lord. And whatever you do in word or deed, do all in the name of the Lord Jesus, giving thanks to God the Father through Him.

We are to cleanse ourselves and worship God from a pure heart. Flesh cannot worship God. If we rid ourselves of all that is not of God, there will be nothing left but our spirits worshiping the Spirit of God.

ABRAHAM, OUR FIRST EXAMPLE

Abraham Worshiped

The first biblical reference to worship is in connection with Abraham.

Genesis 22:5 And Abraham said to his young men, "Stay here with the donkey; the lad and I will go yonder and worship, and we will come back to you."

Law of First Mention

There is a principle of biblical interpretation that is called the "law of first mention." It states that the first biblical mention of any subject gives a clear indication of its meaning and significance wherever else it may occur in the Bible.

The first occurrence of the word "worship" is found when Abraham was speaking to the young men who accompanied Isaac and him to Moriah.

The seriousness of worship is shown by this first mention.

Abraham Obeyed

Abraham's response to God's commandment was one of obedience.

There is no way for us to imagine what obedience to this command demanded of Abraham. Isaac was the promised son. He was the fulfillment of the covenant God had made with Abraham.

Intense Sacrifice

The act of worship at this time was certainly an act of intense sacrifice. This act of worship would demand of Abraham his very best, the highest offering he could possibly make.

The act of worship may still be one of great personal sacrifice.

Romans 12:1,2 I beseech you therefore, brethren, by the mercies of God, that you present your bodies a living sacrifice, holy, acceptable to God, which is your reasonable service. And do not be conformed to this world, but be transformed by the renewing of your mind, that you may prove what is that good and acceptable and perfect will of God.

True worship means that there has been a complete surrender of one's whole self to God.

Act of Obedience – Faith

The act of worship is an act of obedience and faith. Abraham certainly could not have felt like worshiping.

On the third day of his journey to offer Isaac, Abraham said, "We will come back to you."

An act of obedience had turned to an act of faith.

Surrender of Self

The death of Isaac would mean the death of everything Abraham had lived for. Every promise in the Covenant was based on the birth of his son. Everything he had believed was involved with Isaac. It was an act of total surrender to God.

Because of Abraham's obedience to worship, God inhabited that praise and brought a special gift of faith that compelled Abraham to commit to Isaac's sacrifice.

Psalm 22:3 But You are holy, Who inhabit the praises of Israel.

Abraham brought his son to be sacrificed and this became a pattern of ultimate sacrifice. Later, we see the Father allowing the sacrifice of his Son, Jesus. There is even a strong possibility that Jesus was sacrificed at the exact place where Abraham offered Isaac.

We must surrender all personal desires, ambitions, and plans to enter into real worship.

A BENEFIT OF PRAISE

Saul

> *Troubled by Evil Spirits*

1 Samuel 16:14-17,23 But the Spirit of the LORD departed from Saul, and a distressing spirit from the LORD troubled him.

And Saul's servants said to him, "Surely, a distressing spirit from God is troubling you. Let our master now command your servants, who are before you, to seek out a man who is a skillful player on

the harp; and it shall be that he will play it with his hand when the distressing spirit from God is upon you, and you shall be well."

So Saul said to his servants, "Provide me now a man who can play well, and bring him to me."

➤ *Music Brought Deliverance*

Whenever the distressing spirit came on Saul, David would take his harp and play. Then relief would come to Saul; he would feel better, and the distressing spirit would leave him.

Well means skillfully. Musicians and singers should be skillful. Saul's servants knew to seek a skilled musician because they had seen the power of anointed music before. David was chosen.

QUESTIONS FOR REVIEW

1. Write your definition, or understanding, of praise.

2. Write your definition, or understanding, of worship.

3. What characterized Abraham's act of worship as he was to offer his son Isaac as a sacrifice?

God's Pattern for Worship

Worship in Tabernacle

Another principle of biblical interpretation is the "law of much mention." This principle says that the amount of space given a particular subject indicates its importance.

Fifty-one chapters in the Old Testament are devoted to the tabernacles, showing their importance to us.

REVIEW OF TABERNACLES AND TEMPLES IN OLD TESTAMENT

There are several tabernacles and temples mentioned in the Old Testament. Since these were the places where the people met with God, where they entered into His Presence, it is important that we have a basic understanding of them and the difference between them.

Tabernacle of Moses

The pattern, or blueprint, for the Tabernacle of Moses was given in exact detail by God. Tabernacle means a tent and it was in use as the children of Israel moved through the wilderness.

The Tabernacle of Moses was the place of Old Testament worship. It was the temporary dwelling place of the Ark of the Covenant. It was there the Presence of God dwelt and the priest ministered before the Lord. Often when the children of Israel turned to sin, the Ark would be captured by their enemies.

Moses' Tabernacle came to settle in Shiloh.

David's Tabernacle

Because David was a man of war, God did not allow him to build the temple. God gave the plans for the temple to him, and David gathered the materials from which the temple was built.

The Ark of the Covenant resided in David's Tabernacle after it was returned by the Philistines and before Solomon's Temple was built.

The primary purpose of the Tabernacle of David was to demonstrate the worship of God in a unique way.

The Tabernacle of David can be seen as a "window" looking into New Testament worship. The window is framed by a typical Old Testament tent or tabernacle, but the inside was completely different. The priests entered the gates with thanksgiving and the courts with praise because the Ark of God's Presence was in full view. There was no Holy of Holies with its concealing veil and the only sacrifice offered was the sacrifice of praise.

This "window" lasted forty years until Solomon's Temple was built. Then the window was closed and the Ark of the Covenant was transferred to Solomon's Temple. The animal sacrifices were resumed.

Solomon's Temple

Solomon's Temple was designed much like Moses' Tabernacle. It was to have been the final residence of the Ark of the Covenant. The staves for moving the Ark were taken away. This was a permanent dwelling, made of marble and gold, not a temporary tent.

However, over the years, Solomon's Temple was allowed to fall into disrepair. When Israel was defeated and foreign kings would demand high tributes to be paid, the golden vessels were taken from the Temple to meet these demands. The gold was stripped from the walls, columns, and doors. At one time Manasseh built altars to false gods in the Temple, huts were built to house the sodomite activities in the Temple courts and "sacred" horses were stabled in the inner court.

Finally, Solomon's Temple was completely destroyed by the Chaldeans who took everything of value to Babylon and then burned the Temple to the ground.

Zerubbabel's Temple

This Temple was built about 520 B.C. and was not as grand as Solomon's Temple but was larger. It lacked much of the furniture that was in Solomon's Temple. The Ark of the Covenant had been lost.

Herod's Temple

When Herod gained control of Judah he rebuilt Zerubbabel's Temple. Herod did not build from a heart of worship. He had a passion for building and built many magnificent buildings during his reign. The Temple of Zerubbabel was simply not majestic enough for his tastes. It was from Herod's Temple that Jesus came and went. All of the priestly duties were in function and it was here that Jesus overthrew the tables of the moneychangers.

Matthew 21:12,13 Then Jesus went into the temple of God and drove out all those who bought and sold in the temple, and overturned the tables of the moneychangers and the seats of those who sold doves.

And He said to them, "It is written, 'My house shall be called a house of prayer,' but you have made it a 'den of thieves.' "

When Jesus died on the Cross, the veil between the Holy Place and the Holy of Holies (much like a six inch thick rug) was supernaturally torn from top to bottom.

Throughout the history of the Jewish race, only the High Priest could go from the Holy Place into the Holy of Holies. The Holy of Holies was the place where the Ark of the Covenant was kept. It was the place where the Presence of God dwelt. The veil tore from top to bottom signifying that the separation between God and man was removed. Mankind now has the privilege of coming into the Presence of God!

Jesus prophesied that not one brick would remain on another from this Temple and it was destroyed by the Romans in 70 A.D. The Temple and the surrounding buildings were burned completely and as they were burning, the gold melted and flowed into the cracks between the stones. To retrieve the gold, the stones were taken down, thus fulfilling Jesus' prophecy.

Matthew 24:2 And Jesus said to them, "Do you not see all these things? Assuredly, I say to you, not one stone shall be left here upon another, that shall not be thrown down."

FOLLOWING THE ARK

The Ark resided in the Tabernacle of Moses until the time of Eli. It was then stolen as a result of judgment upon Eli's house.

1 Samuel 2:30-32a Therefore the LORD God of Israel says: 'I said indeed that your house and the house of your father would walk before Me forever'; but now the LORD says: 'Far be it from Me; for those who honor Me I will honor, and those who despise Me shall be lightly esteemed. Behold, the days are coming that I will cut off your arm and the arm of your father's house, so that there will not be an old man in your house. And you will see an enemy in My habitation ...

'And what happens to your two sons, Hophni and Phinehas, will be a sign to you–they will both die on the same day. I will raise up for myself a faithful priest, who will do according to what is in my heart and mind. I will firmly establish his house, and he will minister before my anointed one always.'

The Ark of the Covenant was stolen by the Philistines during battle and as it was carried around the land of the Philistines, it brought judgment and disaster upon them wherever it went.

1 Samuel 5:1-4,6-7 Then the Philistines took the ark of God and brought it from Ebenezer to Ashdod. When the Philistines took the ark of God, they brought it into the temple of Dagon and set it by Dagon. And when the people of Ashdod arose early in the morning, there was Dagon, fallen on its face to the earth before the ark of the LORD.

So they took Dagon and set it in its place again. And when they arose early the next morning, there was Dagon, fallen on its face to the ground before the ark of the LORD. The head of Dagon and both the palms of its hands were broken off on the threshold; only the torso of Dagon was left of it.

But the hand of the LORD was heavy on the people of Ashdod, and He ravaged them and struck them with tumors, both Ashdod and its territory. And when the men of Ashdod saw how it was, they said, "The ark of the God of Israel must not remain with us, for His hand is harsh toward us and Dagon our god."

Ark Sent to Jerusalem

Because of God's judgment, the Philistines called their priests together and asked how the Ark should be returned. There was no driver and a team of cows with their calves just taken from them would in the natural follow the calves. Instead, the team of cows went directly to the land of Israel.

God allowed the Philistines to move the Ark on a cart. There were no dedicated men to carry it. But see what happened when God's people tried to do the same thing.

1 Samuel 6:7,8 Now therefore, make a new cart, take two milk cows which have never been yoked, and hitch the cows to the cart; and take their calves home, away from them. Then take the ark of the LORD and set it on the cart; and put the articles of gold which you are returning to Him as a trespass offering in a chest by its side. Then send it away, and let it go.

Warning for Us

David wanted to move the Ark from Kirjath-Jearim to Mount Zion and there is a strong warning in his first attempt to move the Ark.

I Chronicles 13:7,8,10 So they carried the ark of God on a new cart from the house of Abinadab, and Uzza and Ahio drove the cart.

Then David and all Israel played music before God with all their might, with singing, on harps, on stringed instruments, on tambourines, on cymbals, and with trumpets.

Then the anger of the LORD was aroused against Uzza, and He struck him because he put his hand to the ark; and he died there before God.

There was disobedience to God's procedures which were known and practiced. David was responsible, just as we are for proper "temple procedure."

Praise Can't Hide Disobedience

David and his men used a cart to move the Ark, but God had commanded that the Ark be moved by Levites carrying it on their shoulders with wooden staves. The Presence of God could not be carried on a cart. It could only be carried by dedicated, set apart men.

David and all Israel were singing and playing musical instruments before the Lord, but they were in disobedience and death was the result.

The Ark was successfully moved later in obedience to God's instruction.

1 Chronicles 15:2 Then David said, "No one may carry the ark of God but the Levites, for the LORD has chosen them to carry the ark of God and to minister before Him forever."

Just because we desire the Presence of the Lord in our worship does not mean we can do it "our way." The Presence of the Lord must be ushered in as He leads each time. The same "cart" that worked last week, the same songs, tempo, order, etc., will not necessarily work this week.

PRAISE IN DAVID'S TABERNACLE

Praise was an important part of worship in the Tabernacle.

David brought the Ark to Zion and placed it in a tent which we call the Tabernacle of David.

It is interesting to note that God did not direct David to place the Ark in the Tabernacle of Moses, but for the rest of David's life, and until Solomon's Temple was built, the Ark of God's Presence resided in the Tabernacle of David.

1 Chronicles 16:1,4-9,31,34 So they brought the ark of God, and set it in the midst of the tabernacle that David had erected for it. Then they offered burnt offerings and peace offerings before God.

And he appointed some of the Levites to minister before the ark of the LORD, to commemorate, to thank, and to praise the LORD God of Israel ... Jeiel with stringed instruments and harps, but Asaph made music with cymbals; Benaiah and Jahaziel the priests regularly blew the trumpets before the ark of the covenant of God.

And on that day David first delivered this psalm into the hand of Asaph and his brethren, to thank the LORD.

Oh, give thanks to the LORD! Call upon His name;
  make known His deeds among the peoples!
Sing to Him, sing psalms to Him;
  talk of all His wondrous works!

Let the heavens rejoice, and let the earth be glad;
  and let them say among the nations, "The LORD reigns."

Oh, give thanks to the LORD, for He is good!
For His mercy endures forever.

Instruments for Worship

There were many instruments used in worship in David's Tabernacle.

Psalms 150:1-6 Praise the LORD! Praise God in His sanctuary;
  praise Him in His mighty firmament!
Praise Him for His mighty acts;
  praise Him according to His excellent greatness!
Praise Him with the sound of the trumpet;
  praise Him with the lute and harp!
Praise Him with the timbrel and dance;
  praise Him with stringed instruments and flutes!
Praise Him with loud cymbals;
  praise Him with high sounding cymbals!
Let everything that has breath praise the LORD.
Praise the LORD!

In this one short psalm, David listed seven instruments which were to be used in praise to God. The final, and most important "instrument" is our voice.

> ➤ *trumpet*

> ➤ *harp*

> ➤ *lyre*

> ➤ *tambourine*

> ➤ *strings*

> ➤ *flute*

> ➤ *cymbals*

Power of Praise and Worship

> ➤ *Glory Cloud*

When the Ark was brought from David's Tabernacle to Solomon's Temple, the priests and the people praised the Lord until His glory filled the Temple.

2 Chronicles 5:13,14 Indeed it came to pass, when the trumpeters and singers were as one, to make one sound to be heard in praising and thanking the LORD, and when they lifted up their voice with the trumpets and cymbals and instruments of music,

and praised the LORD, saying: "For He is good, for His mercy endures forever," that the house, the house of the LORD, was filled with a cloud, so that the priests could not continue ministering because of the cloud; for the glory of the LORD filled the house of God.

Pattern for Church

Because the Ark of the Covenant was allowed to be seen for forty years, the Tabernacle of David is a pattern of the church corporately and individually worshipping God.

Acts 15:16,17 'After this I will return and will rebuild the tabernacle of David which has fallen down. I will rebuild its ruins, and I will set it up, so that the rest of mankind may seek the Lord, even all the Gentiles who are called by My name, says the Lord who does all these things.'

James was quoting the prophet, Amos, in this scripture.

Amos 9:11,12 "On that day I will raise up the tabernacle of David, which has fallen down, and repair its damages; I will raise up its ruins, and rebuild it as in the days of old; that they may possess the remnant of Edom, and all the Gentiles who are called by My name," says the LORD who does this thing.

God is restoring, spiritually, the Tabernacle of David. Surely He will restore all forms of worship ascribed to that Tabernacle in the body of Christ.

QUESTIONS FOR REVIEW

1. In David's time his Tabernacle was a literal tent, what is David's Tabernacle today?

2. When King David was attempting to move the ark the first time, why did Uzzah die?

3. How is the Tabernacle of Moses different from the Tabernacle of David in representing a pattern of worship?

Lesson Three

God's Instructions for Praise

The Scriptures are full of God's instructions to His people on becoming praisers and worshipers of Him. It is important to spend time reading from His Word so that we will know:

➤ *Why we should praise Him*

➤ *Who should praise Him*

➤ *When we should praise Him*

➤ *Where we should praise Him*

WHY SHOULD WE PRAISE THE LORD?

Because He Is

➤ *Worthy of Thanks*

> Psalms 107:1,2,8 Oh, give thanks to the LORD, for He is good! For His mercy endures forever. Let the redeemed of the LORD say so, whom He has redeemed from the hand of the enemy.
>
> Oh, that men would give thanks to the LORD for His goodness, and for His wonderful works to the children of men!

➤ *Worthy of Praise*

> 2 Samuel 22:4 I will call upon the LORD, who is worthy to be praised; so shall I be saved from my enemies.

➤ *Great*

> Psalm 48:1 Great is the LORD, and greatly to be praised in the city of our God, in His holy mountain.
>
> Psalm 96:4 For the LORD is great and greatly to be praised; He is to be feared above all gods.

➤ *Mighty in Acts*

> Psalm 150:2 Praise Him for His mighty acts; praise Him according to His excellent greatness!

He is the ultimate authority, the highest power. He is before all things, and greater than all things.

Chose Us

> Luke 10:20 Nevertheless do not rejoice in this, that the spirits are subject to you, but rather rejoice because your names are written in heaven.

➤ *To Glorify God*

Psalm 50:23 Whoever offers praise glorifies Me; and to him who orders his conduct aright I will show the salvation of God.

Psalm 69:30 I will praise the name of God with a song, and will magnify Him with thanksgiving.

Commanded to Praise

➤ *Through David*

Psalm 149:1 Praise the LORD! Sing to the LORD a new song, and His praise in the congregation of saints.

➤ *Through Paul*

Ephesians 5:19 Speaking to one another in psalms and hymns and spiritual songs, singing and making melody in your heart to the Lord ...

➤ *Through John*

Revelation 19:5 Then a voice came from the throne, saying, "Praise our God, all you His servants and those who fear Him, both small and great!"

Because It's Good

Psalms 92:1,2 It is good to give thanks to the LORD, and to sing praises to Your name, O Most High; to declare Your lovingkindness in the morning, and Your faithfulness every night.

Because It's Pleasant

Psalm 147:1 Praise the LORD! For it is good to sing praises to our God; for it is pleasant, and praise is beautiful.

Because It's Beautiful

Psalm 33:1 Rejoice in the LORD, O you righteous! For praise from the upright is beautiful.

There is a fear of praising God for some, because they do not feel it is dignified. This is contrary to the Word of God.

2 Samuel 6:14-16,21-23 Then David danced before the LORD with all his might; and David was wearing a linen ephod. So David and all the house of Israel brought up the ark of the LORD with shouting and with the sound of the trumpet.

And as the ark of the LORD came into the City of David, Michal, Saul's daughter, looked through a window and saw King David leaping and whirling before the LORD; and she despised him in her heart.

So David said to Michal, "It was before the LORD, who chose me instead of your father and all his house, to appoint me ruler over the people of the LORD, over Israel. Therefore I will play music before the LORD. And I will be even more undignified than this, and will be humble in my own sight. But as for the maid servants of whom you have spoken, by them I will be held in honor."

Therefore Michal the daughter of Saul had no children to the day of her death.

God Dwells in Praise

Psalm 22:3 But You are holy, Who inhabit the praises of Israel.

If our heart is filled with praise, it is filled with God. If our home is filled with praise, it is filled with God.

We can surround ourselves with the Presence of God by surrounding ourselves with praise.

Praise Releases Strength

Nehemiah 8:10b Do not sorrow, for the joy of the LORD is your strength.

Psalm 28:7 The LORD is my strength and my shield; my heart trusted in Him, and I am helped; therefore my heart greatly rejoices, and with my song I will praise Him.

Praise Brings Fulfillment

The praising soul enjoys being with the Lord, and God gives him the longings of his heart.

Psalm 37:4 Delight yourself also in the LORD, and He shall give you the desires of your heart.

Notice that praise is to come first, before we receive. That's because praise puts our priorities in order, and then God can grant us the desires of our heart.

Praise Brings Victory

Psalm 18:3 I will call upon the LORD, who is worthy to be praised; so shall I be saved from my enemies.

2 Chronicles 20:21,22 And when he had consulted with the people, he appointed those who should sing to the LORD, and who should praise the beauty of holiness, as they went out before the army and were saying: "Praise the LORD, for His mercy endures forever."

Now when they began to sing and to praise, the LORD set ambushes against the people of Ammon, Moab, and Mount Seir, who had come against Judah; and they were defeated.

Even in the everyday battles of life, praise leads the way to victory.

WHO SHOULD PRAISE THE LORD?

All Flesh

> Psalm 145:21b And all flesh shall bless His holy name forever and ever.

My Soul

> Psalms 103:1,2 Bless the LORD, O my soul; and all that is within me, bless His holy name! Bless the LORD, O my soul, and forget not all His benefits.

Everything with Breath

> Psalm 150:6 Let everything that has breath praise the LORD. Praise the LORD!

All the People

> Psalms 67:3,5 Let the peoples praise You, O God; let all the peoples praise You. Let the peoples praise You, O God; let all the peoples praise You.

> Psalm 78:4 We will not hide them from their children, telling to the generation to come the praises of the LORD, and His strength and His wonderful works that He has done.

> Psalm 79:13 So we, Your people and sheep of Your pasture, will give You thanks forever; we will show forth Your praise to all generations.

The Righteous

> Psalm 140:13 Surely the righteous shall give thanks to Your name; the upright shall dwell in Your presence.

The Saints

> Psalm 145:10 All Your works shall praise You, O LORD, and Your saints shall bless You.

The Redeemed

> Psalms 107:1,2 Oh, give thanks to the LORD, for He is good! For His mercy endures forever. Let the redeemed of the LORD say so, whom He has redeemed from the hand of the enemy.

Those Who Fear the Lord

> Psalm 22:23 You who fear the LORD, praise Him! All you descendants of Jacob, glorify Him, and fear Him, all you offspring of Israel!

Servants of God

> Psalm 113:1 Praise the LORD! Praise, O servants of the LORD, Praise the name of the LORD!

> Psalm 134:1 Behold, bless the LORD, all you servants of the LORD, who by night stand in the house of the LORD!

> Psalm 135:1 Praise the LORD! Praise the name of the LORD; praise Him, O you servants of the LORD!

All His Angels

> Psalm 148:2 Praise Him, all His angels; praise Him, all His hosts!

All Nature

> Psalms 148:7-10 Praise the LORD from the earth, you great sea creatures and all the depths; fire and hail, snow and clouds; stormy wind, fulfilling His word; mountains and all hills; fruitful trees and all cedars; beasts and all cattle; creeping things and flying fowl.

Kings and Peoples

> Psalms 148:11-13 Kings of the earth and all peoples; princes and all judges of the earth; both young men and maidens; old men and children. Let them praise the name of the LORD, for His name alone is exalted; His glory is above the earth and heaven.

WHEN ARE WE TO PRAISE THE LORD?

From Morning to Night

> Psalm 113:3 From the rising of the sun to its going down the Lord's name is to be praised.

All Day

> Psalm 71:8 Let my mouth be filled with Your praise and with Your glory all the day.

While We Live

> Psalm 146:2 While I live I will praise the LORD; I will sing praises to my God while I have my being.

Continually

> Psalm 34:1 I will bless the LORD at all times; His praise shall continually be in my mouth.

When Downcast

> Psalm 42:11 Why are you cast down, O my soul? And why are you disquieted within me? Hope in God; for I shall yet praise Him, the help of my countenance and my God.

Always

> Ephesians 5:20 Giving thanks always for all things to God the Father in the name of our Lord Jesus Christ.

WHERE ARE WE TO PRAISE THE LORD?

In the Congregation

> Psalms 22:22,25 I will declare Your name to My brethren; in the midst of the congregation I will praise You.
>
> My praise shall be of You in the great congregation; I will pay My vows before those who fear Him.
>
> Psalm 107:32 Let them exalt Him also in the congregation of the people, and praise Him in the assembly of the elders.

Psalm 149:1 Praise the LORD! Sing to the LORD a new song, and His praise in the congregation of saints.

In the Sanctuary

Psalm 150:1 Praise the LORD! Praise God in His sanctuary; praise Him in His mighty firmament!

Among the Nations

Psalm 57:9 I will praise You, O Lord, among the peoples; I will sing to You among the nations.

In His Courts

Psalm 100:4 Enter into His gates with thanksgiving, and into His courts with praise. Be thankful to Him, and bless His name.

Among the Multitudes

Psalm 109:30 I will greatly praise the LORD with my mouth; yes, I will praise Him among the multitude.

QUESTIONS FOR REVIEW

1. Give three reasons why we should praise the Lord.

2. When are we to praise the Lord? Give one example from scripture and one from your own experience.

3. List three scriptures that you are going to memorize that will either encourage yourself or others to praise God.

Lesson Four

Praise Brings God's Blessings

PRAISE IS LIKENED TO THE RAIN CYCLE

Hydrological Cycle

There are many places in Scripture where praise is likened to the water cycle. This cycle is unending, a continuous cycle flowing from one to the other.

> ➤ *Water on earth evaporates*
>
> ➤ *Forms clouds in the air*
>
> ➤ *Rains back to earth*

Cycle of Praise

Praise is to be just as unending. We give praises to God and our praise brings:

> ➤ *Blessings*
>
> ➤ *Victory*
>
> ➤ *Growth*

Amos 5:8 He made the Pleiades and Orion; He turns the shadow of death into morning and makes the day dark as night; He calls for the waters of the sea and pours them out on the face of the earth; the LORD is His name.

Amos 9:6 He who builds His layers in the sky, and has founded His strata in the earth; who calls for the waters of the sea, and pours them out on the face of the earth–the LORD is His name.

God Pours out Blessings

Just as God calls for the water to evaporate so that it can rain, He calls for us to praise Him so that He can pour out His blessings.

Job 36:27,28 For He draws up drops of water, which distill as rain from the mist, which the clouds drop down and pour abundantly on man.

Hosea 6:3 Let us know, let us pursue the knowledge of the LORD. His going forth is established as the morning; He will come to us like the rain, like the latter and former rain to the earth.

Isaiah 45:8 Rain down, you heavens, from above, and let the skies pour down righteousness; let the earth open, let them bring forth salvation, and let righteousness spring up together. I, the LORD, have created it.

**Praises Go Up
Blessings Come Down**

As we send praises to God, He turns them to blessings to rain back on us.

Proverbs 11:25 The generous soul will be made rich, and he who waters will also be watered himself.

Psalms 67:5,6 Let the peoples praise You, O God; let all the peoples praise You. Then the earth shall yield her increase; God, our own God, shall bless us.

Psalms 147:7,8 Sing to the LORD with thanksgiving; sing praises on the harp to our God, Who covers the heavens with clouds, Who prepares rain for the earth, Who makes grass to grow on the mountains.

Zechariah 10:1 Ask the LORD for rain in the time of the latter rain. the LORD will make flashing clouds; He will give them showers of rain, grass in the field for everyone.

Unending Cycle

James 5:7 Therefore be patient, brethren, until the coming of the Lord. See how the farmer waits for the precious fruit of the earth, waiting patiently for it until it receives the early and latter rain.

Just as the farmer doesn't reap in the same season that he sows, be patient, for in time you will reap your harvest, or blessing.

God causes His blessings to shine on mankind just as the sun shines upon the ocean. Man's heart should be warmed towards God in response to the blessings He has shone upon him.

Man's praises are to arise to God just as the vapors that are created by the sun on the ocean.

Those praises form clouds of blessing.

God causes them to distill into rain which pours forth on the earth.

The excess rain forms rivers which run to the sea, from whence it originally came, and the whole process begins again.

BENEFITS OF PRAISE

Releases God To Act

Acts 16:25,26 But at midnight Paul and Silas were praying and singing hymns to God, and the prisoners were listening to them. Suddenly there was a great earthquake, so that the foundations of the prison were shaken; and immediately all the doors were opened and everyone's chains were loosed.

Earth Yields Increase

Psalms 67:5,6 Let the peoples praise You, O God; let all the peoples praise You. Then the earth shall yield her increase; God, our own God, shall bless us.

Victory Comes

2 Chronicles 20:21,22 And when he had consulted with the people, he appointed those who should sing to the LORD, and who should praise the beauty of holiness, as they went out before the army and were saying: "Praise the LORD, for His mercy endures forever."

Now when they began to sing and to praise, the LORD set ambushes against the people of Ammon, Moab, and Mount Seir, who had come against Judah; and they were defeated.

Brings Health

Proverbs 17:22 A merry heart does good, like medicine, but a broken spirit dries the bones.

Brings Peace

Isaiah 60:18 Violence shall no longer be heard in your land, neither wasting nor destruction within your borders; but you shall call your walls Salvation, and your gates Praise.

Changes Us

We are changed into the same glory as the God we worship.

2 Corinthians 3:11,18 For if what is passing away was glorious, what remains is much more glorious.

But we all, with unveiled face, beholding as in a mirror the glory of the Lord, are being transformed into the same image from glory to glory, just as by the Spirit of the Lord.

1 John 3:1,2 Behold what manner of love the Father has bestowed on us, that we should be called children of God! Therefore the world does not know us, because it did not know Him. Beloved, now we are children of God; and it has not yet been revealed what we shall be, but we know that when He is revealed, we shall be like Him, for we shall see Him as He is.

REJOICING IN THE LORD

A Sad Face

A sad countenance is an expression of an ungrateful heart.

Nehemiah 2:1,2 And it came to pass in the month of Nisan, in the twentieth year of King Artaxerxes, when wine was before him, that I took the wine and gave it to the king. Now I had never been sad in his presence before.

Therefore the king said to me, "Why is your face sad, since you are not sick? This is nothing but sorrow of heart."

Then I became dreadfully afraid.

When the king recognized the sorrow in Nehemiah's face, Nehemiah was afraid. A sad face could mean that he was unhappy in the king's service, and could mean his death.

To come into the king's presence in an unhappy mood was an insult. To come into the Presence of God with an unhappy expression is to indicate that we are unhappy with the things He has:

➢ *Given us*

➢ *Done for us*

➢ *Provided for us*

➢ *Planned for us*

Commanded to Rejoice

We are commanded to rejoice before the Lord.

Deuteronomy 12:7,11,12 And there you shall eat before the LORD your God, and you shall rejoice in all to which you have put your hand, you and your households, in which the LORD your God has blessed you, then there will be the place where the LORD your God chooses to make His name abide.

There you shall bring all that I command you: your burnt offer- ings, your sacrifices, your tithes, the heave offerings of your hand, and all your choice offerings which you vow to the LORD. And you shall rejoice before the LORD your God, you and your sons and your daughters, your menservants and your maidservants, and the Levite who is within your gates, since he has no portion nor inheritance with you.

1 Chronicles 16:10 Glory in His holy name; let the hearts of those rejoice who seek the LORD!

Psalm 33:1 Rejoice in the LORD, O you righteous! For praise from the upright is beautiful.

Luke 1:46,47 And Mary said: "My soul magnifies the Lord, and my spirit has rejoiced in God my Savior."

Philippians 4:4 Rejoice in the Lord always. Again I will say, rejoice!

Joy and Rejoicing Come

Joy and rejoicing come from the revelation and meditation of God's Word.

Jeremiah 15:16 Your words were found, and I ate them, and Your word was to me the joy and rejoicing of my heart; for I am called by Your name, O LORD God of hosts.

After Seed Is Sown

We are to "go out with joy" after the seed of God's Word is sown in our hearts.

Isaiah 55:10-12 For as the rain comes down, and the snow from heaven, and do not return there, but water the earth, and make it bring forth and bud, that it may give seed to the sower and bread to the eater, so shall My word be that goes forth from My mouth; it shall not return to Me void, but it shall accomplish what I please, and it shall prosper in the thing for which I sent it.

For you shall go out with joy, and be led out with peace; the mountains and the hills shall break forth into singing before you, and all the trees of the field shall clap their hands.

Stop Satan with Joy

What does Satan try to do after the Word has been sown in our hearts? He comes immediately with his afflictions and persecutions to steal that seed.

If we become offended and lose our joy, we allow Satan to steal the seed of the Word which has been sown in our heart.

Mark 4:4,14-17 And it happened, as he sowed, that some seed fell by the wayside; and the birds of the air came and devoured it.

The sower sows the word. And these are the ones by the wayside where the word is sown. And when they hear, Satan comes immediately and takes away the word that was sown in their hearts.

These likewise are the ones sown on stony ground who, when they hear the word, immediately receive it with gladness; and they have no root in themselves, and so endure only for a time. Afterward, when tribulation or persecution arises for the word's sake, immediately they stumble.

Joy Produces Fruit

The seed of His Word will abide in us as His joy remains in us.

John 15:10,11 If you keep My commandments, you will abide in My love, just as I have kept My Father's commandments and abide in His love. These things I have spoken to you, that My joy may remain in you, and that your joy may be full.

Through obedience to God's Word, His joy will remain in us. His joy is not temporary, partial, or circumstantial. It is complete.

Hebrews 10:32-34 But recall the former days in which, after you were illuminated, you endured a great struggle with sufferings: partly while you were made a spectacle both by reproaches and tribulations, and partly while you became companions of those who were so treated; for you had compassion on me in my chains, and joyfully accepted the plundering of your goods, knowing that you have a better and an enduring possession for yourselves in heaven.

1 Peter 4:12,13 Beloved, do not think it strange concerning the fiery trial which is to try you, as though some strange thing happened to you; but rejoice to the extent that you partake of Christ's sufferings, that when His glory is revealed, you may also be glad with exceeding joy.

Matthew 5:11,12 Blessed are you when they revile and persecute you, and say all kinds of evil against you falsely for My sake. Rejoice and be exceedingly glad, for great is your reward in heaven, for so they persecuted the prophets who were before you.

John 16:22 Therefore you now have sorrow; but I will see you again and your heart will rejoice, and your joy no one will take from you.

Joy Brings Strength

As we rejoice and praise the Lord, we receive His strength.

Nehemiah 8:10b Do not sorrow, for the joy of the LORD is your strength.

Joy Overcomes Evil One

Rejoicing is the key to overcoming "the evil one" (Satan).

As we rejoice and keep the seed of His Word, we are strong and victorious in our Christian life.

1 John 2:13,14 I write to you, fathers, because you have known him who is from the beginning. I write to you, young men, because you have overcome the wicked one. I write to you, little children, because you have known the Father. I have written to you, fathers, because you have known Him who is from the beginning. I have written to you, young men, because you are strong, and the word of God abides in you, and you have overcome the wicked one.

Joy Brings Restoration

If Satan has stolen our joy and we have lost the seed of the Word, our goods and our victory, we can get them all back.

As we raise our voice in joy and offer the sacrifices of praise in the house of the Lord, our captivity will be returned and Satan must return all that he has stolen.

Jeremiah 33:9-11 Then it shall be to Me a name of joy, a praise, and an honor before all nations of the earth, who shall hear all the good that I do to them; they shall fear and tremble for all the goodness and all the prosperity that I provide for it.

Thus says the LORD: 'Again there shall be heard in this place–of which you say, "It is desolate, without man and without beast"– in the cities of Judah, in the streets of Jerusalem that are desolate, without man and without inhabitant and without beast, the voice of joy and the voice of gladness, the voice of the bridegroom and the voice of the bride, the voice of those who will say:

"Praise the LORD of hosts, for the LORD is good, for His mercy endures forever"–and of those who will bring the sacrifice of praise into the house of the LORD. For I will cause the captives of the land to return as at the first,' says the LORD.

Must Repay Sevenfold

As we rejoice, we can demand that the thief (Satan) repay us sevenfold all that he has stolen.

John 10:10 The thief does not come except to steal, and to kill, and to destroy. I have come that they may have life, and that they may have it more abundantly.

Proverbs 6:30,31 People do not despise a thief if he steals to satisfy himself when he is starving. Yet when he is found, he must restore sevenfold; he may have to give up all the substance of his house.

Let's Start Rejoicing Right Now!

QUESTIONS FOR REVIEW

1. Describe how praise is similar to the hydrological cycle.

2. List two benefits of praise.

3. Name two things that "joy in the Lord" can do.

Biblical Words of Praise

WORDS TRANSLATED PRAISE IN OLD TESTAMENT

A number of different and distinctive Hebrew words were used to describe praise in the Old Testament. A study of these words reveals a clearer understanding of what it means to praise God today.

Hebrew words for praise express much excitement and action.

Halal

Halal is the most frequently used word translated as praise. It occurs 160 times in the Old Testament.

It means: His praise coming from Him (in spirit and truth)

➢ *To Make a Show*

Psalm 22:22 I will declare Your name to My brethren; in the midst of the congregation I will praise You.

➢ *To Boast*

Psalm 102:18 This will be written for the generation to come, that a people yet to be created may praise the LORD.

➢ *To Celebrate*

Psalm 35:18 I will give You thanks in the great congregation; I will praise You among many people.

➢ *To Rave About*

Psalm 107:32 Let them exalt Him also in the congregation of the people, and praise Him in the assembly of the elders.

➢ *To Glory In*

Psalm 64:10 The righteous shall be glad in the LORD, and trust in Him. And all the upright in heart shall glory.

➢ *To Shine*

Job 41:18 His sneezings flash forth light, and his eyes are like the eyelids of the morning.

True praise, therefore, should have a clear and distinct sound. There should be no confusion as to what is intended. It is a note of celebration, a boasting in the Lord.

2 Chronicles 20:21,22 And when he had consulted with the people, he appointed those who should sing to the LORD, and who

should praise the beauty of holiness, as they went out before the army and were saying:

"Praise the LORD, for His mercy endures forever."

Now when they began to sing and to praise, the LORD set ambushes against the people of Ammon, Moab, and Mount Seir, who had come against Judah; and they were defeated.

Tehillah
(A Derivative of Halal)

The emphasis of the word tehillah is on singing. It is used fifty-seven times in the Old Testament.

➢ *Sing Clear Song of Praise*

It means to sing forth a clear song of praise to God.

Psalm 119:171 My lips shall utter praise, for You teach me Your statutes.

➢ *Celebrate Him in Song*

Habakkuk 3:3 God came from Teman, the Holy One from Mount Paran. Selah His glory covered the heavens, and the earth was full of His praise.

➢ *To Boast About*

We are to boast about Him in words and music.

Deuteronomy 10:21 He is your praise, and He is your God, who has done for you these great and awesome things which your eyes have seen.

Shabach
➢ *To Shout with Loud Voice*

Psalm 63:3 Because Your lovingkindness is better than life, my lips shall praise You.

➢ *To Shout in Triumph*

Daniel 2:23 I thank You and praise You, O God of my fathers; you have given me wisdom and might, and have now made known to me what we asked of You, for You have made known to us the king's demand.

➢ *To Glory in Victory*

Psalm 117:1 Oh, praise the LORD, all you Gentiles! Laud Him, all you peoples!

Praise does not always need to be noisy. We do not always need to shout, but there are times when it is the only fitting manner of praise to God.

Psalm 47:1 Oh, clap your hands, all you peoples! Shout to God with the voice of triumph!

Zamar

Zamar means:

➤ *To touch or play the strings*

➤ *Also has sense of singing praise to the accompaniment of musical instruments*

Psalm 108:1-3 O God, my heart is steadfast; I will sing and give praise, even with my glory. Awake, lute and harp! I will awaken the dawn. I will praise You, O LORD, among the peoples, and I will sing praises to You among the nations.

Yadah

Yadah means:

➤ *To give forth a confession of thanks*

Psalm 109:30 I will greatly praise the LORD with my mouth; yes, I will praise Him among the multitude.

➤ *Also has thought of giving thanks with the hands extended towards God*

Psalm 33:2 Praise the LORD with the harp; make melody to Him with an instrument of ten strings.

➤ *Submission*

2 Chronicles 7:3 When all the children of Israel saw how the fire came down, and the glory of the LORD on the temple, they bowed their faces to the ground on the pavement, and worshiped and praised the LORD, saying: "For He is good, for His mercy endures forever."

Towdah

Towdah comes from the same root as yadah and means:

➤ *The extension of the hands in adoration and thanksgiving*

Psalm 42:4 When I remember these things, I pour out my soul within me. For I used to go with the multitude; I went with them to the house of God, with the voice of joy and praise, with a multitude that kept a pilgrim feast.

➤ *Sacrifice by acknowledgment in reverence*

Psalm 50:23 Whoever offers praise glorifies Me; and to him who orders his conduct aright I will show the salvation of God.

Barak

Barak means:

➤ *To kneel in adoration*

Psalm 95:6b ... let us kneel before the LORD our Maker.

To kneel before someone is to manifest humility and to demonstrate their superior worth and position.

Shachah

While several Hebrews words were translated "worship," only one Hebrew word was used in the Old Testament to express worship toward God.

➤ *To Bow Low*

Shachah means to bow one's self down before God in worship and adoration. It also expressed an attitude of the heart, even if the person's body was not prostrated.

Psalm 95:6a Oh come, let us worship and bow down.

DISCOVERIES ON PRAISE AND WORSHIP FROM HEBREW WORDS

Physical Expression

Praise is a physical expression of spiritual attitudes, an inner response of the heart to a revelation of God and His greatness.

There is often a physical action – praise is something we do. It includes making a show, celebrating, glorying in, raving, playing instruments, raising hands and kneeling.

To be true praise, it must be manifested.

Vocal Expression

Much of praise involves vocal expression. The Hebrew words describe: clear songs of praise, producing a clear sound, boasting, singing, shouting with a loud voice, giving a triumphant shout and giving confessions of thanks to God.

Emotional Release

Praise can be an emotional release.

Praising God is not an emotional exercise; it is a spiritual activity.

True praise will bring emotional release.

Emotions are not necessarily carnal, or fleshly.

God gave us emotions, and they are to be used to glorify Him. The emotions include celebrating, raving and giving expression by shouting loudly.

Reverence

Praise should be done in an attitude of reverence. Reverence means to honor and esteem someone properly.

Activities of praise should never be allowed to degenerate into excesses outside of the boundaries of the anointing and flow of the Holy Spirit in that particular meeting.

Praising God is not merely a means of enjoying ourselves, it should be offered as an expression of reverence and thanksgiving toward God.

Conclusions

We can draw some conclusions from the Hebrew words.

God is a Spirit and we are to worship Him in spirit and in truth.

Praise may be emotional, but we must guard against praise being simply an enjoyment of the flesh and not being given in the spirit.

John 4:23,24 But the hour is coming, and now is, when the true worshipers will worship the Father in spirit and truth; for the Father is seeking such to worship Him. God is Spirit, and those who worship Him must worship in spirit and truth.

WORDS TRANSLATED PRAISE AND WORSHIP IN NEW TESTAMENT

Several Greek words were used to describe praise in the New Testament. A study of these words will release us to be more active and expressive in our praise to God.

Aineo
  ➢ *Praise Offering or Celebration*

Romans 15:11 And again: "Praise the Lord, all you Gentiles! Laud Him, all you peoples!"

  ➢ *Lifting of Voice in Thanks*

Luke 19:37 Then, as He was now drawing near the descent of the Mount of Olives, the whole multitude of the disciples began to rejoice and praise God with a loud voice for all the mighty works they had seen.

Epaineo
  ➢ *To Applaud*

1 Peter 1:7 That the genuineness of your faith, being much more precious than gold that perishes, though it is tested by fire, may be found to praise, honor, and glory at the revelation of Jesus Christ.

  ➢ *To Commend for*

Ephesians 1:6 To the praise of the glory of His grace, by which He has made us accepted in the Beloved.

Eulogeo
> *To Speak Well of*

Luke 1:64 Immediately his mouth was opened and his tongue loosed, and he spoke, praising God.

Doxa
> *Glorious*

Doxa denotes more of the atmosphere created by worship than the physical expressions.

John 9:24a So they again called the man who was blind, and said to him, "Give God the glory!"

Proskuneo
> *Bow Down*

Proskuneo means "to prostrate oneself in homage."

Matthew 2:2 Saying, "Where is He who has been born King of the Jews? For we have seen His star in the East and have come to worship Him."

DEFINITIONS OF PRAISE AND WORSHIP TERMS

Psalm

Psalm comes from the Greek word, psalmos. It's general meaning is "poems composed to be sung."

Psalmos

Psalmos is a psalm with musical accompaniment. It originally meant "striking, or twitching, with the fingers on musical strings as with a harp."

Hymn

Hymn is from the Greek word, humnas, meaning a song of praise to God, or from the Greek word, humneo meaning "to sing a song of praise addressed to God."

Spiritual Song

The Greek words, pneumatikos ode (spiritual song) means, "a spontaneous song with the words and music given at that time by the Holy Spirit."

QUESTIONS FOR REVIEW

1. List two words from the Old Testament that are translated as praise and define their meaning from the Hebrew language.
2. List two New Testament words for praise. Give their meaning from the Greek language.
3. What was the meaning of the Hebrew word that was used for worship to God.
4. Give the meaning of the two Greek words that were translated as worship.

Lesson Six

God's Eternal Purpose for Praise

We were created for praise and worship. The greatest desires of our life should be to praise and worship God. The reason we live should be to worship Him. John tells us that God is seeking for sons and daughters to worship Him!

John 4:23 But the hour is coming, and now is, when the true worshipers will worship the Father in spirit and truth; for the Father is seeking such to worship Him.

God Rejoices with Singing

God Himself rejoices over us with singing!

Zephaniah 3:17 The LORD your God in your midst, the Mighty One, will save; He will rejoice over you with gladness, He will quiet you in His love, He will rejoice over you with singing.

The Hebrew word used to describe God's actions in rejoicing means "to jump up and down and spin around in jubilant excitement."

We could ask, "Why is God so thrilled with us that He is rejoicing, jumping up and down in jubilant excitement? To understand the answer to this question, we need to go back to Eternity Past, and understand the function of praise and worship by the angels.

ANGELS CREATED

The angels were created by God for definite functions. The multitude of angels seem to have been divided under the leadership of three major angels.

> ➢ *The archangel Michael was the leader of the large, warrior angels.*

> ➢ *The angel Gabriel was the leader of the messenger angels.*

> ➢ *The angel Lucifer was the leader of the angels created specifically for praise and worship as a covering of the throne of God.*

Lucifer

> *Anointed Cherub*

God created the angel Lucifer as the guardian cherub that protected the throne of God.

Ezekiel 28:14 You were the anointed cherub who covers; I established you; you were on the holy mountain of God; you walked back and forth in the midst of fiery stones.

As the cherubs covered the mercy seat over the Ark of the Covenant with their wings even so Lucifer was next to the throne of God as the "anointed cherub who covers."

> *Meaning of Name*

In Hebrew, Lucifer is "heylel." It comes from the root word "halal," from which we get "hallelujah." It means to praise, be bright, shine, be splendid, celebrate, glorify and be famous. The name, Lucifer is a good indication that his primary function was praise and worship.

Lucifer was the original "hallelujah," the original praiser who celebrated and shone with the reflected, radiant, glory of the Lord. We can all agree with Isaiah when He wrote:

Isaiah 14:12a How you are fallen from heaven, O Lucifer, son of the morning!

> *Created for Music*

Ezekiel 28:13b The workmanship of your timbrels and pipes was prepared for you on the day you were created.

Lucifer did not just play an instrument, he was one. His voice was an orchestra with percussion instruments, flutes, horns and voice.

Lucifer was also adorned with so many gems that when he moved and breathed it was a never-ending, always changing, spectacle of glory in light and heavenly sound.

Notice that all of the three major types of musical instruments – percussion, wind and stringed – are mentioned.

The covering of the throne of God by the anointed cherub appears to have been a covering of praise and worship.

Lucifer must have led the great angelic orchestra and choir in praise and worship continually before the throne.

Job 38:7 When the morning stars sang together, and all the sons of God shouted for joy?

LUCIFER LEFT VOID

The fall of Lucifer from heaven left a huge void. When Lucifer rebelled against God and was cast out of heaven, "his angels," a third part of the stars (angels) of heaven who rebelled, left with him.

Isaiah 14:12 How you are fallen from heaven, O Lucifer, son of the morning! How you are cut down to the ground, you who weakened the nations!

Ezekiel 28:15,16 You were perfect in your ways from the day you were created, till iniquity was found in you. By the abundance of your trading you became filled with violence within, and you sinned; therefore I cast you as a profane thing out of the mountain of God; and I destroyed you, O covering cherub, from the midst of the fiery stones.

Revelation 12:7-9 And war broke out in heaven: Michael and his angels fought against the dragon; and the dragon and his angels fought, but they did not prevail, nor was a place found for them in heaven any longer. So the great dragon was cast out, that serpent of old, called the Devil and Satan, who deceives the whole world; he was cast to the earth, and his angels were cast out with him.

Revelation 12:4a His tail drew a third of the stars of heaven and threw them to the earth.

A void was suddenly realized in heaven as Lucifer and his angels were cast out.

God Filled Void

God had a plan to fill the void left by Lucifer and his angels! God created man to take dominion on this earth over Lucifer (Satan) and his angels (demons). Man was to demonstrate Satan's defeat on this earth. God created man to be next to Him and reign with Him on His throne.

The void is now filled.

Ephesians 1:23 Which is His body, the fullness of Him who fills all in all.

The church, composed of all the men and women who are believers, is to take the place of the guardian cherub and his angels. The church is now next to the throne of God.

Man was created for one great purpose and function – to praise and worship God!

Ephesians 3:21 To Him be glory in the church by Christ Jesus throughout all ages, world without end. Amen.

SATAN AND MUSIC

Lucifer the Chief Musician

Before his fall, Lucifer was a chief musician in heaven.

Ezekiel 28:13b The workmanship of your timbrels and pipes was prepared for you on the day you were created.

His gift of music was to be used in praise to God, but when he fell, this gift became perverted.

Instruments Invented

Descendants of Cain invented both instruments of music and instruments of war.

Genesis 4:21,22a His brother's name was Jubal. He was the father of all those who play the harp and flute. And as for Zillah, she also bore Tubal-Cain, an instructor of every craftsman in bronze and iron.

Confusion in Music

Satan is the author of confusion and confusion in music is a sign that it's satanic.

1 Corinthians 14:33a For God is not the author of confusion but of peace ...

➢ *Golden Calf*

When the children of Israel had made the calf and were worshiping it, Moses heard a sound so confusing that he could not at first discern the significance of it.

Exodus 32:17,18 And when Joshua heard the noise of the people as they shouted, he said to Moses, "There is a noise of war in the camp."

But he said: "It is not the voice of those who shout in victory, nor is it the voice of those who cry out in defeat, but the voice of those who sing that I hear."

➢ *Golden Image*

Nebuchadnezzar used musical instruments of various kinds to induce the worship of the golden image he erected.

Daniel 3:5,7 ... at the time you hear the sound of the horn, flute, harp, lyre, and psaltery, in symphony with all kinds of music, you shall fall down and worship the gold image that King Nebuchadnezzar has set up ...

So at that time, when all the people heard the sound of the horn, flute, harp, and lyre, in symphony with all kinds of music, all the people, nations, and languages fell down and worshiped the gold image which King Nebuchadnezzar had set up.

YOUR WILL BE DONE ON EARTH AS IT IS IN HEAVEN

Jesus taught His disciples to pray, **Your will be done on earth as it is in heaven.** What is God's will in heaven? What is being done there?

John was given a tremendous vision of what is happening in heaven today, and of what is going to happen in the future. Much of this vision included praise and worship.

Continuous Praise

The angelic beings are continuously giving praise to God.

Revelation 4:8-11 And the four living creatures ... do not rest day or night, saying: "Holy, holy, holy, Lord God Almighty, Who was and is and is to come!"

Whenever the living creatures give glory and honor and thanks to Him who sits on the throne, who lives forever and ever, the twenty-four elders fall down before Him who sits on the throne and worship Him who lives forever and ever, and cast their crowns before the throne, saying: "You are worthy, O Lord, to receive glory and honor and power; for You created all things, and by Your will they exist and were created."

Thousands upon Thousands

There are over one hundred million angels and creatures worshiping and praising God.

Revelation 5:11-13 Then I looked, and I heard the voice of many angels around the throne, the living creatures, and the elders; and the number of them was ten thousand times ten thousand, and thousands of thousands, saying with a loud voice: "Worthy is the Lamb who was slain to receive power and riches and wisdom, and strength and honor and glory and blessing!"

And every creature which is in heaven and on the earth and under the earth and such as are in the sea, and all that are in them, I heard saying: "Blessing and honor and glory and power be to Him who sits on the throne, and to the Lamb, forever and ever!"

Jesus prayed, **Your will be done on earth as it is in heaven.**

Total Worship

There is total praise and worship going on in heaven now. Worship by the thousands of angels and worship by a multitude of people from every nation, tribe, and language.

Revelation 7:9,10 After these things I looked, and behold, a great multitude which no one could number, of all nations, tribes, peoples, and tongues, standing before the throne and before the Lamb, clothed with white robes, with palm branches in their hands, and crying out with a loud voice, saying, "Salvation belongs to our God who sits on the throne, and to the Lamb!"

Jesus taught the disciples to pray, **Your will be done on earth as it is in heaven.**

With New Songs

Revelation 14:1-3 Then I looked, and behold, a Lamb standing on Mount Zion, and with Him one hundred and forty-four thousand, having His Father's name written on their foreheads. And I heard a voice from heaven, like the voice of many waters, and like the voice of loud thunder. And I heard the sound of harpists playing their harps. And they sang as it were a new song before the throne, before the four living creatures, and the elders; and no one could learn that song except the hundred and forty-four thousand who were redeemed from the earth.

We are to pray, **Your will be done on earth as it is in heaven.**

Future Worship

John saw the saints, and that includes us, worshiping God after the complete destruction of Satan.

Revelation 15:2-4 And I saw something like a sea of glass mingled with fire, and those who have the victory over the beast, over his image and over his mark and over the number of his name, standing on the sea of glass, having harps of God. And they sing the song of Moses, the servant of God, and the song of the Lamb, saying:

"Great and marvelous are Your works, Lord God Almighty! Just and true are Your ways, O King of the saints! Who shall not fear You, O Lord, and glorify Your name? For You alone are holy. For all nations shall come and worship before You, for Your judgments have been manifested."

Revelation 19:1,3,7 After these things I heard a loud voice of a great multitude in heaven, saying, "Alleluia! Salvation and glory and honor and power to the Lord our God!" Again they said, "Alleluia! And her smoke rises up forever and ever! Let us be glad and rejoice and give Him glory, for the marriage of the Lamb has come, and His wife has made herself ready."

Now it is up to us, His bride, to make ourselves ready by being praisers and worshipers of God. John continued, **Let us be glad and rejoice and give Him glory, for the marriage of the Lamb has come, and His wife has made herself ready.**

QUESTIONS FOR REVIEW

1. Who was created to lead worship in heaven? Explain your answer.

2. Who filled the void of the former worship leader? Explain.

3. Is all music inspired by God? How can you tell the difference?

Music, an Expression of Worship

MUSICAL INSTRUMENTS

Musical instruments were frequently used to express praise and worship.

By David

Psalms 150:3-5 Praise Him with the sound of the trumpet; praise Him with the lute and harp! Praise Him with the timbrel and dance; praise Him with stringed instruments and flutes! Praise Him with loud cymbals; praise Him with high sounding cymbals!

Musicians who would offer praises on their instruments must seek to excel in doing so.

Psalm 33:3 Sing to Him a new song; play skillfully with a shout of joy.

This may be a spiritual skill, rather then natural talent. Skill is not only in playing the instrument, but in discerning and expressing the flow and feeling of the Spirit.

David's skillful playing on the harp drove the distressing spirits from Saul and brought refreshment and healing.

1 Samuel 16:23 And so it was, whenever the spirit from God was upon Saul, that David would take a harp and play it with his hand. Then Saul would become refreshed and well, and the distressing spirit would depart from him.

By Priests

1 Chronicles 23:5 Four thousand were gatekeepers, and four thousand praised the LORD with musical instruments, "which I made," said David, "for giving praise."

In Heaven

Revelation 14:2 And I heard a voice from heaven, like the voice of many waters, and like the voice of loud thunder. And I heard the sound of harpists playing their harps.

HOLY SPIRIT INSPIRES MUSIC

Releases Anointing

The Holy Spirit can use music for the glory of God and for the edification of people. Music can help create an atmosphere for the gifts of tongues, interpretation of tongues, prophecy, healing, words of knowledge and wisdom, the gift of faith and working of miracles.

2 Kings 3:15,16a But now bring me a musician. And it happened, when the musician played, that the hand of the LORD came upon him.

An Expression of Freedom

➤ *In Captivity*

When Israel was in captivity their music ceased.

Psalms 137:1-4 By the rivers of Babylon, there we sat down, yea, we wept when we remembered Zion. We hung our harps upon the willows in the midst of it. For there those who carried us away captive required of us a song, and those who plundered us required of us mirth, saying, "Sing us one of the songs of Zion!" How shall we sing the Lord's song in a foreign land?

➤ *In Freedom*

When their captivity ceased, after seventy years, they returned home with joyful singing and laughter.

Psalms 126:1,2 When the LORD brought back the captivity of Zion, we were like those who dream. Then our mouth was filled with laughter, and our tongue with singing. Then they said among the nations, "The LORD has done great things for them."

MUSIC IN PRAISE AND WORSHIP IN OLD TESTAMENT

First Mention

Genesis 4:21 His brother's name was Jubal. He was the father of all those who play the harp and flute.

The name, Yabal, or Jubal (Hebrew) means to flow with pomp as a stream. It is associated with the expression of mirth.

Moses

Moses and the children of Israel sang unto the Lord.

Exodus 15:1,2 Then Moses and the children of Israel sang this song to the LORD, and spoke, saying: "I will sing to the LORD, for He has triumphed gloriously! The horse and its rider He has thrown into the sea! The LORD is my strength and song, and He has become my salvation; He is my God, and I will praise Him; my father's God, and I will exalt Him."

Miriam

Miriam and all the women responded to the song of the Lord that Miriam sang.

Exodus 15:20,21 Then Miriam the prophetess, the sister of Aaron, took the timbrel in her hand; and all the women went out after her with timbrels and with dances. And Miriam answered them: "Sing to the LORD, for He has triumphed gloriously! The horse and its rider He has thrown into the sea!"

Israelites

The Israelites celebrated with song.

Numbers 21:17 Then Israel sang this song: "Spring up, O well! all of you sing to it ..."

Deborah and Barak

Deborah and Barak celebrated their victory with song.

Judges 5:1-3 Then Deborah and Barak the son of Abinoam sang on that day, saying: "When leaders lead in Israel, when the people willingly offer themselves, bless the LORD! Hear, O kings! Give ear, O princes! I, even I, will sing to the LORD; I will sing praise to the LORD God of Israel."

Women of Israel

Women of Israel celebrated David's victory over Goliath.

1 Samuel 18:6,7 Now it had happened as they were coming home, when David was returning from the slaughter of the Philistine, that the women had come out of all the cities of Israel, singing and dancing, to meet King Saul, with tambourines, with joy, and with musical instruments. So the women sang as they danced, and said: "Saul has slain his thousands, and David his ten thousands."

David

David was continually singing praises to the Lord.

Psalm 7:17 I will praise the LORD according to His righteousness, and will sing praise to the name of the LORD Most High.

Psalm 13:6 I will sing to the LORD, because He has dealt bountifully with me.

Psalm 21:13 Be exalted, O LORD, in Your own strength! We will sing and praise Your power.

Priests

4,000 Levites praised the Lord with instruments.

1 Chronicles 15:16 Then David spoke to the leaders of the Levites to appoint their brethren to be the singers accompanied by instruments of music, stringed instruments, harps, and cymbals, by raising the voice with resounding joy.

1 Chronicles 23:5 Four thousand were gatekeepers, and four thousand praised the LORD with musical instruments, "which I made," said David, "for giving praise."

2 Chronicles 30:21 So the children of Israel who were present at Jerusalem kept the Feast of Unleavened Bread seven days with great gladness; and the Levites and the priests praised the LORD day by day, singing to the LORD, accompanied by loud instruments.

MUSIC IN PRAISE AND WORSHIP IN NEW TESTAMENT

Disciples

The disciples sang songs together.

Matthew 26:30 And when they had sung a hymn, they went out to the Mount of Olives.

A hymn was a song of praise toward God.

Paul

Paul instructed the church in anointed singing.

1 Corinthians 14:15 What is the result then? I will pray with the spirit, and I will also pray with the understanding. I will sing with the spirit, and I will also sing with the understanding.

Ephesians 5:19,20 Speaking to one another in psalms and hymns and spiritual songs, singing and making melody in your heart to the Lord, giving thanks always for all things to God the Father in the name of our Lord Jesus Christ.

Colossians 3:16 Let the word of Christ dwell in you richly in all wisdom, teaching and admonishing one another in psalms and hymns and spiritual songs, singing with grace in your hearts to the Lord.

Hymns

Hymns are songs of praise to God.

Spiritual Songs

Spiritual songs are songs given directly by the Holy Spirit and sung spontaneously as the Spirit supplies both the words and melody.

They may be in the language of the person singing, or in an unknown tongue.

Main Objective

The primary objective in singing was to praise and magnify God. They did not sing for effect, or to entertain. Their singing was not man-centered. It was directed to God for His pleasure alone.

Hebrews 2:12 Saying: "I will declare Your name to My brethren; in the midst of the congregation I will sing praise to You."

SPIRITUAL EXPRESSIONS OF PRAISE

Praising God with Voice

1 Chronicles 16:9 Sing to Him, sing psalms to Him; talk of all His wondrous works!

Psalms 71:23,24 My lips shall greatly rejoice when I sing to You, and my soul, which You have redeemed. My tongue also shall talk of Your righteousness all the day long; for they are confounded, for they are brought to shame Who seek my hurt.

➤ *Make it a habit to talk to the Lord.*

➤ *Extol his wonderful works.*

➤ *Begin each day speaking His praises.*

➤ *Praise Him with speaking and with singing.*

➤ *Cultivate the habit of praise.*

Psalm 40:16 Let all those who seek You rejoice and be glad in You; let such as love Your salvation say continually, "The LORD be magnified!"

Psalm 66:8 Oh, bless our God, you peoples! And make the voice of His praise to be heard.

Praising the Lord may be with singing, as a spontaneous expression of joyful emotion. It can also be what we say. Praise is a healthy expression of positive emotions which ministers strength to the total being.

Shouting unto God

There is a time to speak, and a time to shout.

Psalm 47:1 Oh, clap your hands, all you peoples! Shout to God with the voice of triumph!

Isaiah 12:6 Cry out and shout, O inhabitant of Zion, for great is the Holy One of Israel in your midst!

1 Samuel 4:5 And when the ark of the covenant of the LORD came into the camp, all Israel shouted so loudly that the earth shook.

Luke 19:37 Then, as He was now drawing near the descent of the Mount of Olives, the whole multitude of the disciples began to rejoice and praise God with a loud voice for all the mighty works they had seen.

QUESTIONS FOR REVIEW

1. Give scriptural examples of musical instruments being used in praise.
2. Give scriptural examples of music releasing the anointing to prophesy.
3. Give an example of music being used in praise and worship in the Old Testament.
4. Give an example of music being used in praise and worship in the New Testament.

Lesson Eight

Physical Expressions of Praise

Note: Songs should be selected prior to beginning this lesson which will be most effective in activating the physical expressions of praise, one-by-one, as they are studied. After each physical expression is studied, take time to experience that particular expression in a time of high praise or intimate worship. It is amazing how the presence of God will come into our midst as we experience each of the biblical expressions of praise and worship.

PHYSICAL EXPRESSIONS OF PRAISE

Standing

Standing is a sign of respect.

2 Chronicles 20:19 Then the Levites of the children of the Kohathites and of the children of the Korahites stood up to praise the LORD God of Israel with voices loud and high.

Revelation 7:9,10 After these things I looked, and behold, a great multitude which no one could number, of all nations, tribes, peoples, and tongues, standing before the throne and before the Lamb, clothed with white robes, with palm branches in their hands, and crying out with a loud voice, saying, "Salvation belongs to our God who sits on the throne, and to the Lamb!"

Psalm 33:8 Let all the earth fear the LORD; let all the inhabitants of the world stand in awe of Him.

Psalms 135:1,2 Praise the LORD! Praise the name of the LORD; praise Him, O you servants of the LORD! You who stand in the house of the LORD, in the courts of the house of our God.

Clapping Hands

Clapping your hands is an expression of gladness, rejoicing and approval.

Psalm 47:1 Oh, clap your hands, all you peoples! Shout to God with the voice of triumph!

Isaiah 55:12 For you shall go out with joy, and be led out with peace; the mountains and the hills shall break forth into singing before you, and all the trees of the field shall clap their hands.

Marching

Marching is a physical expression of overcoming victory. Marching around Jericho, as commanded, brought complete victory.

Joshua 6:2-5 And the LORD said to Joshua: "See! I have given Jericho into your hand, its king, and the mighty men of valor. You shall march around the city, all you men of war; you shall go all

around the city once. This you shall do six days. And seven priests shall bear seven trumpets of rams' horns before the ark.

But the seventh day you shall march around the city seven times, and the priests shall blow the trumpets. Then it shall come to pass, when they make a long blast with the ram's horn, and when you hear the sound of the trumpet, that all the people shall shout with a great shout; then the wall of the city will fall down flat. And the people shall go up every man straight before him."

The Bride of Christ is pictured as an army marching forward together.

Song of Solomon 6:4,10 O my love, you are as beautiful as Tirzah, lovely as Jerusalem, awesome as an army with banners! Who is she who looks forth as the morning, fair as the moon, clear as the sun, awesome as an army with banners?

Dancing

Dancing is the most demonstrative of the physical expressions of praise. It requires the use of the whole body. It involves a complete and total release of ones own inhibitions and self-consciousness as we obey God and dance before Him with all our might.

Psalm 149:3 Let them praise His name with the dance; let them sing praises to Him with the timbrel and harp.

2 Samuel 6:14 Then David danced before the LORD with all his might ...

We will study more about dancing at the end of this lesson.

Laughter

There is an expression of such joy in the Lord that the only way to express it is through laughter. Great healing and deliverance often comes during times of holy laughter before the Lord. True laughter is a manifestation of inner joy.

Psalm 126:2 Then our mouth was filled with laughter, and our tongue with singing. Then they said among the nations, "The LORD has done great things for them."

Job 8:20,21 Behold, God will not cast away the blameless, nor will He uphold the evildoers. He will yet fill your mouth with laughing, and your lips with rejoicing.

PHYSICAL EXPRESSIONS OF WORSHIP

Lifting Hands

In the natural realm, raising your hands is a sign of surrender. In worship, it is a sign of sacrifice and surrender.

Romans 12:1 I beseech you therefore, brethren, by the mercies of God, that you present your bodies a living sacrifice, holy, acceptable to God, which is your reasonable service.

Psalm 141:2 Let my prayer be set before You as incense, the lifting up of my hands as the evening sacrifice.

It is a reaching out and thirsting after God

Psalm 143:6 I spread out my hands to You; my soul longs for You like a thirsty land. Selah

Psalms 42:1,2 As the deer pants for the water brooks, so pants my soul for You, O God. My soul thirsts for God, for the living God. When shall I come and appear before God?

Raising your hands can also be an act of blessing God.

Psalm 134:2 Lift up your hands in the sanctuary, and bless the LORD.

Psalm 63:4 Thus I will bless You while I live; I will lift up my hands in Your name.

Raising your hands may be a physical expression of prayer and supplication.

Psalm 28:2 Hear the voice of my supplications when I cry to You, when I lift up my hands toward Your holy sanctuary.

1 Timothy 2:8 Therefore I desire that the men pray everywhere, lifting up holy hands, without wrath and doubting.

Bowing or Kneeling

Bowing down or kneeling is a gesture of reverence and respect.

Psalm 95:6 Oh come, let us worship and bow down; let us kneel before the LORD our Maker.

Falling Prostrate

Falling face-down on the floor is an expression of deepest respect and worship, of absolute reverence, a complete humbling of one's self.

1 Kings 18:39 Now when all the people saw it, they fell on their faces; and they said, "The LORD, He is God! The LORD, He is God!"

1 Chronicles 29:20 Then David said to all the congregation, "Now bless the LORD your God." So all the congregation blessed the

LORD God of their fathers, and bowed their heads and prostrated themselves before the LORD and the king.

Silence

Silence can be an expression of praise.

Ecclesiastes 3:7 A time to tear, and a time to sew; a time to keep silence, and a time to speak ...

Psalm 46:10 Be still, and know that I am God; I will be exalted among the nations, I will be exalted in the earth!

Tears

Tears are often a response to experiencing the intense love and compassion of God.

Acts 20:36,37 And when he had said these things, he knelt down and prayed with them all. Then they all wept freely, and fell on Paul's neck and kissed him.

Tears accompanying praise are an expression of overwhelming gratitude and adoration. They often bring a deep emotional release and inner healing.

Luke 7:37,38 And behold, a woman in the city who was a sinner, when she knew that Jesus sat at the table in the Pharisee's house, brought an alabaster flask of fragrant oil and stood at His feet behind Him weeping; and she began to wash His feet with her tears, and wiped them with the hair of her head; and she kissed His feet and anointed them with the fragrant oil.

Tears often precede great joy and victory.

Psalms 126:5,6 Those who sow in tears shall reap in joy. He who continually goes forth weeping, bearing seed for sowing, shall doubtless come again with rejoicing, bringing his sheaves with him.

DANCING

Dancing is not more important than the other expressions of praise. However, it is more controversial and thus needs more explanation than some of the other forms.

Definition

Dancing is highly demonstrative. It requires the use of the whole body in order to express joy, praise and worship before the Lord.

Hebrew and Greek words translated "dance" mean "leaping, skipping, lifting up the feet, jumping." In other words, something spontaneous and unstructured in nature.

Acts 3:8 So he, leaping up, stood and walked and entered the temple with them walking, leaping, and praising God.

Psalm 149:3 Let them praise His name with the dance; let them sing praises to Him with the timbrel and harp.

OLD TESTAMENT EXAMPLES OF DANCING

In Celebration

The children of Israel danced to celebrate salvation and deliverance when they were delivered from the Egyptians.

Exodus 15:20 Then Miriam the prophetess, the sister of Aaron, took the timbrel in her hand; and all the women went out after her with timbrels and with dances.

They rejoiced when the ark of the covenant was being restored.

2 Samuel 6:14 Then David danced before the LORD with all his might ...

Spiritual Dance

The spiritual dance is spontaneous, primitive and unsophisticated in style and can be expressed in skipping, whirling, leaping and jumping. It is sometimes accompanied by music from instruments and by singing.

Psalm 149:3 Let them praise His name with the dance; let them sing praises to Him with the timbrel and harp.

➤ *By Individual or Group*

David danced before the Lord.

Miriam and all the women danced.

The spiritual dance is not dancing with a member of the opposite sex.

> ➤ *Miriam and all the women danced*

> ➤ *Young men and the old together*

Jeremiah 31:13a Then shall the virgin rejoice in the dance, and the young men and the old, together ...

➤ *No Age Limit*

There is no age limit on the spiritual dance notice the wording "young men and old."

Singing and Dancing

Singing and dancing often went together.

1 Samuel 29:5 "Is this not David, of whom they sang to one another in dances, saying: 'Saul has slain his thousands, and David his ten thousands'?"

Time to Dance

There is a right time to dance.

Ecclesiastes 3:4 A time to weep, and a time to laugh; a time to mourn, and a time to dance ...

Dancing Before the Lord

This expression of praise is one of obedience to God's revealed Word that we are to praise Him in the dance. As an act of our will, even if we feel awkward in doing so, we obey God and join with other believers as they dance before the Lord.

Dancing in Spirit

Dancing in the spirit is when our whole body is completely under the control of the Holy Spirit. The believers during this time are completely "lost" in the Spirit and so totally absorbed in His power that they are totally unaware of themselves, or others around them. It will always be in God's perfect timing so as not to detract from, but rather be in perfect harmony and flow with the move of God at that moment.

Restoration Prophesied

The restoration of the dance was prophesied.

Jeremiah 31:4,13 Again I will build you, and you shall be rebuilt, O virgin of Israel! You shall again be adorned with your tambourines, and shall go forth in the dances of those who rejoice. Then shall the virgin rejoice in the dance, and the young men and the old, together; for I will turn their mourning to joy, will comfort them, and make them rejoice rather than sorrow.

If we are spiritual Israel, then this is for us today.

WARNINGS

Beware of Carnal Dancing

Dancing of a carnal nature is also associated with backsliding, idolatry, immorality, and worldliness. Satan has a counterfeit for everything. Counterfeits only prove there is a genuine and original.

Not for Show

The purpose of dancing in praise to God was never intended for a "show" or performance that would draw the peoples' attention to the dancers. Instead, the dance is to be a spontaneous and intensely physical expression of praise to God which involves the whole assembly of believers.

It is to be participated in by both women and men, and by both the young and old.

Jeremiah 31:13a Then shall the virgin rejoice in the dance, and the young men and the old, together ...

Believers are not to stop praising and become "observers" or to in any way become distracted from intense praise during the time of "spiritual dance" or "dancing before the Lord." Neither is the dance to be allowed to become a "production" where only a certain select few are performing for the entertainment of others.

While the dance must be a free expression of praise that involves the complete person - spirit, soul, and body - caution must be taken. Our dress and our actions must always be those that will glorify the Lord and not call attention to ourselves.

Enter In

For believers to refuse to enter into the dance of praise before the Lord when the Holy Spirit is moving in that way is an act of rebellion before God. To be self-conscious and fearful of losing one's dignity can grieve or quench the flowing of the Holy Spirit.

Some of the greatest "breakthroughs" happen as the move of the Holy Spirit comes upon a body of believers when each one is dead to self and moves in obedience to the Holy Spirit, doing as David did, "dancing before the Lord with all of his might."

QUESTIONS FOR REVIEW

1. Name three physical expressions of praise that could be interpreted as gestures of reverence and respect.

2. In addition to the tabernacle of David, what physical expression of worship is prophesied to be restored to the church?

3. What physical expression of praise are you most uncomfortable with? What does the Word of God say about that particular aspect? Are you willing to praise God in this way if He wants you to do so?

Lesson Nine

Hindrances to Praise

An inability to enter into praise and worship indicates there is a basic problem between us and God. It is important that each believer seeks Him until they know what their problem, or problems are and then deal with them. The same hindrances that keep us from praising the Lord, can keep us from moving ahead with God, from having our prayers answered, or from being healed.

Excuses Often Given

"I'm just not outgoing!"
"I'm too shy; I feel self-conscious!"
"I'm not demonstrative."

However, praise is a commandment from God and there are no valid excuses!

Psalm 150:6 Let everything that has breath praise the LORD. Praise the LORD!

HINDRANCES TO PRAISE THAT MUST BE DEALT WITH

Sin

Sin breaks our fellowship and communion with God. Sin inhibits us in the Presence of God.

Psalm 66:18 If I regard iniquity in my heart, the Lord will not hear.

Isaiah 59:2 But your iniquities have separated you from your God; and your sins have hidden His face from you, so that He will not hear.

✥ *Solution*

The answer is to confess our sin, or sins, and to accept His forgiveness.

1 John 1:9 If we confess our sins, He is faithful and just to forgive us our sins and to cleanse us from all unrighteousness.

Condemnation

Condemnation is put on us by Satan, never by God.

Once we have asked God to forgive us, we must forgive ourselves. Condemnation of ourselves results in:

> ➤ *Sense of unworthiness – so we tend to "hang our heads" in God's Presence.*

> *Being so conscious of our unworthiness that we forget God's mercy and grace. We become self-conscious instead of God-conscious.*

✍ *Solution*

Romans 8:1 There is therefore now no condemnation to those who are in Christ Jesus, who do not walk according to the flesh, but according to the Spirit.

> *Take thoughts off yourself and put them on Jesus.*

> *The more time we spend thinking about Jesus, the more we will desire to praise Him.*

Hebrews 12:2 Looking unto Jesus, the author and finisher of our faith, who for the joy that was set before Him endured the cross, despising the shame, and has sat down at the right hand of the throne of God.

Worldliness

Worldliness is having our minds and thoughts centered on the things of this world.

Desiring "dignity," or "decorum," more than ministry to God in worship.

✍ *Solution*

1 Peter 5:7 Casting all your care upon Him, for He cares for you.

Philippians 4:8 Finally, brethren, whatever things are true,
whatever things are noble,
whatever things are just,
whatever things are pure,
whatever things are lovely,
whatever things are of good report,
if there is any virtue and if there is anything praiseworthy –
meditate on these things.

1 John 2:15 Do not love the world or the things in the world. If anyone loves the world, the love of the Father is not in him.

Romans 12:2 And do not be conformed to this world, but be transformed by the renewing of your mind, that you may prove what is that good and acceptable and perfect will of God.

Indifference

Being lukewarm or indifferent toward the Lord often hinders a person from entering into praise and worship.

Revelation 2:4 Nevertheless I have this against you, that you have left your first love.

ᣔ *Solution*

Set your heart to return to God in full repentance and then as an act of obedience, begin to praise Him.

Malachi 3:7a "Yet from the days of your fathers you have gone away from My ordinances and have not kept them. Return to Me, and I will return to you," says the LORD of hosts.

Rebellion

Rebellion toward God, parents, or the authority that God has set in the church is a major hindrance to praise.

I Samuel 15:22,23 Then Samuel said: "Has the LORD as great delight in burnt offerings and sacrifices, as in obeying the voice of the LORD? Behold, to obey is better than sacrifice, and to heed than the fat of rams. For rebellion is as the sin of witchcraft, and stubbornness is as iniquity and idolatry. Because you have rejected the word of the LORD, He also has rejected you from being king."

ᣔ *Solution*

Submit to authority and repent of your rebellion.

Hebrews 13:17 Obey those who rule over you, and be submissive, for they watch out for your souls, as those who must give account. Let them do so with joy and not with grief, for that would be unprofitable for you.

Discouragement

Many bring their troubles into church with them. It is important that we prepare our hearts to praise God before we arrive.

2 Corinthians 4:8,9b We are hard pressed on every side, yet not crushed; we are perplexed, but not in despair; persecuted, but not forsaken; struck down, but not destroyed.

ᣔ *Solution*

As we begin in obedience to praise and worship God, all of the discouragement will lift from our hearts.

Isaiah 51:11 So the ransomed of the LORD shall return, and come to Zion with singing, with everlasting joy on their heads; they shall obtain joy and gladness, and sorrow and sighing shall flee away.

Anger

It is impossible to come to God in praise and worship if we are holding anger in our hearts toward others, ourselves, or God.

James 1:19,20b Therefore, my beloved brethren, let every man be swift to hear, slow to speak, slow to wrath; for the wrath of man does not produce the righteousness of God.

✥ *Solution*

Forgive those who have wronged you and refuse to allow the anger to stay in your heart.

Ephesians 4:31,32 Let all bitterness, wrath, anger, clamor, and evil speaking be put away from you, with all malice. And be kind to one another, tenderhearted, forgiving one another, just as God in Christ also forgave you.

Worry

Worry is an expression of doubt and unbelief; the opposite of faith. It is impossible to enter into praise and worship if our thoughts are full of worry.

John 14:27 Peace I leave with you, My peace I give to you; not as the world gives do I give to you. Let not your heart be troubled, neither let it be afraid.

✥ *Solution*

As we focus our eyes on Jesus and the promises of His Word and instead of worrying, begin to thank Him for what He has done and who He is, our hearts will be flooded with peace and the praise will begin to flow from our hearts toward God.

Philippians 4:6,7 Be anxious for nothing, but in everything by prayer and supplication, with thanksgiving, let your requests be made known to God; and the peace of God, which surpasses all understanding, will guard your hearts and minds through Christ Jesus.

Depression

To allow ourselves to become overcome with a spirit of depression because of our circumstances is to stop the flow of praise in our lives.

I Peter 4:12,13 Beloved, do not think it strange concerning the fiery trial which is to try you, as though some strange thing happened to you; but rejoice to the extent that you partake of Christ's sufferings, that when His glory is revealed, you may also be glad with exceeding joy.

✥ *Solution*

As a sacrifice of praise, we must begin to rejoice. As an act of obedience to God, we must put on our garment of praise.

Isaiah 61:3 To console those who mourn in Zion, to give them beauty for ashes, the oil of joy for mourning, the garment of praise for the spirit of heaviness; that they may be called trees of righteousness, the planting of the LORD, that He may be glorified.

Wrong Concept of Father

Many have negative feelings about God. They feel God is always judging them. Others feel God does not want a person to enjoy him or herself.

✍ *Solution*

The answer is to gain a "right" concept of God by spending time in His Word.

John 3:16 For God so loved the world that He gave His only begotten Son, that whoever believes in Him should not perish but have everlasting life.

Romans 8:31,32,38,39 What then shall we say to these things? If God is for us, who can be against us? He who did not spare His own Son, but delivered Him up for us all, how shall He not with Him also freely give us all things? For I am persuaded that neither death nor life, nor angels nor principalities nor powers, nor things present nor things to come, nor height nor depth, nor any other created thing, shall be able to separate us from the love of God which is in Christ Jesus our Lord.

Religious Traditions

Religion oppresses, but redemption releases.

Matthew 15:6b Thus you have made the commandment of God of no effect by your tradition.

✍ *Solution*

The answer is to carefully expose our traditions to the Word of God and to let the Holy Spirit show us the right way.

Pride

Pride is to be overly concerned with our self-image, of wanting to be well thought of. Pride puts man and self on the throne instead of God. Desiring the praises of men is the opposite of giving praise to God.

Jesus described the proud religious leaders of his time.

Matthew 23:1,2,5-7 Then Jesus spoke to the multitudes and to His disciples, Saying: "The scribes and the Pharisees sit in Moses' seat. But all their works they do to be seen by men. They make their phylacteries broad and enlarge the borders of their garments. They love the best places at feasts, the best seats in

the synagogues, greetings in the marketplaces, and to be called by men, 'Rabbi, Rabbi.' "

✎ *Solution*

The solution is to humble yourself.

Matthew 23:11,12 But he who is greatest among you shall be your servant. And whoever exalts himself will be abased, and he who humbles himself will be exalted.

Romans 12:3 For I say, through the grace given to me, to everyone who is among you, not to think of himself more highly than he ought to think, but to think soberly, as God has dealt to each one a measure of faith.

Fear of Man

The fear of what other people think of us is a form of bondage and blocks the Holy Spirit from guiding our actions and attitudes. Fear of man results in worry and anxiety and takes our eyes from the Lord, who He is and who we are to Him.

Fear, of any kind, is the opposite of faith.

Proverbs 29:25 The fear of man brings a snare, but whoever trusts in the LORD shall be safe.

Proverbs 9:10 The fear of the LORD is the beginning of wisdom, and the knowledge of the Holy One is understanding.

✎ *Solution*

When we put God in His rightful place in our lives, when we begin to know Him as He is, the fear of others will disappear.

Satanic Oppression

Satan hates God, therefore he hates praise given to God. He desires all praise to go to him. If you praise God continually, Satan will not stay around!

✎ *Solution*

The solution for heavy oppression is deliverance from demonic bondage.

Mark 16:17a And these signs will follow those who believe: in My name they will cast out demons ...

James 4:7 Therefore submit to God. Resist the devil and he will flee from you.

Ignorance

In many areas, the importance of praise and worship in the lives of believers has been lost.

✠ *Solution*

The solution is to study what God has written on the subject.

Hosea 4:6 My people are destroyed for lack of knowledge. Because you have rejected knowledge, I also will reject you from being priest for Me; because you have forgotten the law of your God, I also will forget your children.

Act! Don't React!

Many have reacted in a negative way to those who have been "in the flesh" during praise and worship. Some believers have reacted and have been "turned off" by the excesses of others. This has become a hindrance to being able to freely enter into all of the biblical expressions of praise and worship.

✠ *Solution*

Instead of reacting to others, we need to act upon God's Word. We need to respond in willful obedience to the revelation of God's Word. We as His children should freely express our heartfelt praise, and worship Him on a continual basis.

To react is to be restricted and held in bondage to religious traditions and fear of man. To act is to be totally free to move and flow with the Spirit of God.

Jesus came to set us free!

John 8:32 And you shall know the truth, and the truth shall make you free.

Conclusion

An inability to praise and worship indicates a basic problem which needs to be dealt with. Seek God until you know the problem and then deal with it honestly. If you still cannot enter into praise to God, go to a mature Christian and seek his or her help.

QUESTIONS FOR REVIEW

1. Name one hindrance to praise and the solution as found in God's Word.

2. Name one hindrance to praise that you have felt within your own life. How have you overcome it, or how are you going to overcome it?

3. What would you do if all of your efforts failed to overcome a hindrance to praise?

Lesson Ten

Offering Sacrifice of Praise

DIFFERENCE BETWEEN PRAISE AND SACRIFICE OF PRAISE

Hebrews 13:15 Therefore by Him let us continually offer the sacrifice of praise to God, that is, the fruit of our lips, giving thanks to His name.

There is a difference between praising God and the sacrifice of praise.

Praise

Praise flows easily when we are in a "right relationship" with God. It is a spontaneous flow when we think of all that He has done for us.

Sacrifice of Praise

The sacrifice of praise is offered to God when things do not seem to be going right. It is:

> ➢ *Praise offered in spite of the way things are going,*

> ➢ *Praise offered in faith and obedience,*

> ➢ *Praise offered because of who God is.*

SACRIFICE OF PRAISE

Continuous

The sacrifice of praise is a continual praise.

Psalm 34:1 I will bless the LORD at all times; His praise shall continually be in my mouth.

Audible

The sacrifice of praise is an audible praise. Several times, David said, **His praise shall continually be in my mouth.**

Paul and Silas – Examples

Paul and Silas in prison praised God in song and miracles followed.

Acts 16:22-26 Then the multitude rose up together against them; and the magistrates tore off their clothes and commanded them to be beaten with rods. And when they had laid many stripes on them, they threw them into prison, commanding the jailer to keep them securely. Having received such a charge, he put them into the inner prison and fastened their feet in the stocks. But at

midnight Paul and Silas were praying and singing hymns to God, and the prisoners were listening to them.

Suddenly there was a great earthquake, so that the foundations of the prison were shaken; and immediately all the doors were opened and everyone's chains were loosed.

➤ *Physical Condition*

They were attacked and persecuted.
Their clothes torn off.
They were beaten,
Thrust into the inner prison with the lowest of criminals,
Locked in stocks to restrain their movements.

➤ *Spiritual Condition*

They were praying and singing hymns.

Did they pray,
"God why did you let this happen?
We were serving you.
We were where you sent us!"

We know they did not! They sang praises and the other prisoners heard them.

➤ *Results*

They were loosed, and subsequently freed.

The jailer and all his "house" were saved.

Everyone in the prison heard about Jesus.

The other believers of Philippi were comforted.

Jehoshaphat – Another Example

Jehoshaphat followed the commandments of God and experienced miraculous victories. His name, Jehos, means "the Lord rules."

➤ *Taught People the Word*

2 Chronicle 17:3-6 Now the LORD was with Jehoshaphat, because he walked in the former ways of his father David; he did not seek the Baals, but sought the God of his father, and walked in His commandments and not according to the acts of Israel. Therefore the LORD established the kingdom in his hand; and all Judah gave presents to Jehoshaphat, and he had riches and honor in abundance. And his heart took delight in the ways of the LORD; moreover he removed the high places and wooden images from Judah.

➤ *Prayed in Time of Trouble*

For years the surrounding nations were afraid of him and left the nation alone, but then they united to come against him. Jehoshaphat came before the assembly and prayed. His prayer started with praise.

2 Chronicles 20:6-9 And said: "O LORD God of our fathers, are You not God in heaven, and do You not rule over all the kingdoms of the nations, and in Your hand is there not power and might, so that no one is able to withstand You? Are You not our God, who drove out the inhabitants of this land before Your people Israel, and gave it to the descendants of Abraham Your friend forever? And they dwell in it, and have built You a sanctuary in it for Your name, saying, 'If disaster comes upon us, such as the sword, judgment, pestilence, or famine, we will stand before this temple and in Your presence (for Your name is in this temple), and cry out to You in our affliction, and You will hear and save.' "

➤ *God Answered*

Then God answered through a prophet.

2 Chronicles 20:15-18 And he said, "Listen, all you of Judah and you inhabitants of Jerusalem, and you, King Jehoshaphat! Thus says the LORD to you: 'Do not be afraid nor dismayed because of this great multitude, for the battle is not yours, but God's. Tomorrow go down against them. They will surely come up by the ascent of Ziz, and you will find them at the end of the brook before the Wilderness of Jeruel. You will not need to fight in this battle. Position yourselves, stand still and see the salvation of the LORD, who is with you, O Judah and Jerusalem!' Do not fear or be dismayed; tomorrow go out against them, for the LORD is with you."

➤ *All Worshiped*

And Jehoshaphat bowed his head with his face to the ground, and all Judah and the inhabitants of Jerusalem bowed before the LORD, worshiping the LORD.

➤ *Appointed Singers*

In preparation for battle, Jehoshaphat appointed men to sing and praise the Lord. These men were stationed at the front of the army!

vs. 21-22 And when he had consulted with the people, he appointed those who should sing to the LORD, and who should praise the beauty of holiness, as they went out before the army and were saying: "Praise the LORD, for His mercy endures forever." Now when they began to sing and to praise, the LORD set ambushes against the people of Ammon, Moab, and Mount Seir, who had come against Judah; and they were defeated.

➤ *Victory*

v. 23 For the people of Ammon and Moab stood up against the inhabitants of Mount Seir to utterly kill and destroy them. And when they had made an end of the inhabitants of Seir, they helped to destroy one another.

vs. 24-26 So when Judah came to a place overlooking the wilderness, they looked toward the multitude; and there were their dead bodies, fallen on the earth. No one had escaped.

When Jehoshaphat and his people came to take away their spoil, they found among them an abundance of valuables on the dead bodies, and precious jewelry, which they stripped off for themselves, more than they could carry away; and they were three days gathering the spoil because there was so much. And on the fourth day they assembled in the Valley of Berachah, for there they blessed the LORD; therefore the name of that place was called The Valley of Berachah until this day.

Summary

> *Physical Condition*

They were being attacked by multitudes from three nations.

> *Spiritual Condition*

They knew what God's Word said. They began to offer praises, not after the enemy was defeated, but while the enemy was surrounding them and everything looked hopeless. They offered a sacrifice of praise.

> *The Result*

The result was complete victory as their enemies killed each other, and they received great spoils.

> *Steps to Victory!*

Through Joshoshaphat we find five steps to victory.

> *Know the Word*

> *Seek God's Presence*

> *Hear From God*

> *Believe the Word and worship God*

> *Act in faith: praise God before the victory is manifested.*

WARFARE IN PRAISE

Great spiritual authority and power is often released in musical expressions of praise to God. The example we have just studied was of Paul and Silas singing songs of praise and then deliverance came by way of a mighty earthquake.

Praise Precedes Victory

When Jehoshaphat appointed men to sing and praise the Lord and they went before the army, a great victory was won. They had used their mighty spiritual weapons and as they were praising God, great power and spiritual authority were released. Often when we are praising God, His Spirit will lead us into songs of spiritual warfare.

Psalms 149:6-9 Let the high praises of God be in their mouth, and a two-edged sword in their hand, to execute vengeance on the nations, and punishments on the peoples.

To bind their kings with chains, and their nobles with fetters of iron; to execute on them the written judgment this honor have all His saints. Praise the LORD!

In spiritual warfare, we not only win as the sharp two-edged sword of God's Word is spoken from our mouths, but great victories are also won in the spirit realm as the praises of God are sung.

Isaiah 30:31,32 For through the voice of the LORD Assyria will be beaten down, who struck with a rod. And in every place where the staff of punishment passes, which the LORD lays on him, it will be with tambourines and harps; and in battles of brandishing He will fight with it.

The music of praise has an important part in winning every spiritual battle.

Worship – Prophecy – Warfare

Revelation 19:6-8 And I heard, as it were, the voice of a great multitude, as the sound of many waters and as the sound of mighty thunderings, saying, "Alleluia! For the Lord God Omnipotent reigns! Let us be glad and rejoice and give Him glory, for the marriage of the Lamb has come, and His wife has made herself ready." And to her it was granted to be arrayed in fine linen, clean and bright, for the fine linen is the righteous acts of the saints.

➢ *Worship*

There is a new sound of praise and worship that is coming to the Church today. It often comes as a roaring sound like mighty rushing waters and loud expressions that sound like thunder and loud shouts of victory. In the roaring sound, Jesus who has before been revealed as the Lamb of God, is now revealed as the Lion of the tribe of Judah.

The apostle John describes the final great battle when Satan will be bound on this earth.

Revelation 19:10,11 And I fell at his feet to worship him. But he said to me, "See that you do not do that! I am your fellow servant, and of your brethren who have the testimony of Jesus. Worship God! For the testimony of Jesus is the spirit of prophecy."

Then I saw heaven opened, and behold, a white horse. And He who sat on him was called Faithful and True, and in righteousness He judges and makes war.

There are three important aspects of this great spiritual battle.

- ➢ *Worship*
- ➢ *Prophecy*
- ➢ *Warfare*

➢ *Prophecy*

Often in praise and worship, a "spirit of prophecy" will be manifested in a "spiritual song" of warfare. Every time this happens great battles are won in the spirit world. There is a binding:

- ➢ *Of principalities*
- ➢ *Powers*
- ➢ *And rulers of darkness*

Psalm 149:8 To bind their kings with chains, and their nobles with fetters of iron ...

➢ *Warfare*

Our passage in Revelation nineteen continues as it gives a description of Jesus and His saints coming back in this great battle of triumph over the devil and his demon powers.

Revelation 19:12-16 His eyes were like a flame of fire, and on His head were many crowns. He had a name written that no one knew except Himself. He was clothed with a robe dipped in blood, and His name is called The Word of God. And the armies in heaven, clothed in fine linen, white and clean, followed Him on white horses.

Now out of His mouth goes a sharp sword, that with it He should strike the nations. And He Himself will rule them with a rod of iron. He Himself treads the winepress of the fierceness and wrath of Almighty God. And He has on His robe and on His thigh a name written: KING OF KINGS AND LORD OF LORDS.

SACRIFICE OF PRAISE OFFERED THROUGH JESUS

Sacrifice of praise can be offered only through Jesus.

Hebrews 13:15 Therefore by Him let us continually offer the sacrifice of praise to God, that is, the fruit of our lips, giving thanks to His name.

It is giving thanks in His Name for who He is and what He has done.

Ephesians 5:20 Giving thanks always for all things to God the Father in the name of our Lord Jesus Christ ...

It is giving thanks in all circumstances, not in just the things we consider good.

1 Thessalonians 5:16-18 Rejoice always, pray without ceasing, in everything give thanks; for this is the will of God in Christ Jesus for you.

We can do this when we fully realize how God can turn all things to work together for good in our lives.

Romans 8:28 And we know that all things work together for good to those who love God, to those who are the called according to His purpose.

Brings Glory to God

The sacrifice of praise brings glory to God.

Psalm 50:23a Whoever offers praise glorifies Me ...

HOW TO OFFER SACRIFICE OF PRAISE

Make Decision

Determine beforehand that you are going to praise God at all times and in every situation.

Start Now

Praise God every day – all day.

Cultivate the habit of praise.

If Trouble Comes

> ➢ *Remember your decision.*
>
> ➢ *Continue in your habit of praise.*
>
> ➢ *Remember that praise in the difficult times allows God to work in your behalf.*
>
> ➢ *Praise in times of trouble brings glory to the Father.*

The time when we do not feel like praising God is the time when we most need to praise Him. As we act in obedience to His Word and begin to praise Him, we are offering the true sacrifice of praise to God and that is well-pleasing to Him.

Begin by Faith

The way you begin to offer the sacrifice of praise is by faith. Praise Him for Who He is and what He has done. Then offer thanks to God for the situation even if you do not understand it.

Praise Him for making a way of deliverance, even though you can see no way out of the problem. Praise God for

Who He is and set your mind on Him and on the promises of His Word.

Once you have started to make the sacrifice of praise – continue. Declare aloud the Word of God that proclaims victory and deliverance.

First you will be offering praise in obedience. By doing this, you will be keeping your mind on Him and not on the circumstance. As you keep comparing His power and glory to your circumstance, you will see how small it actually is.

When you fill your mind with the Word of God and focus on His power and His promises, a spirit of praise replaces the doubts and worries.

Often when it seems difficult to praise, as you start to praise in obedience to God, you will begin to be over-whelmed by the Spirit of praise.

Soon you will find yourself joyfully entering into the full dimension of His Presence as you continue to release your spirit in the sacrifice of praise.

> *Sing unto Him.*

> *Dance before Him.*

> *Glorify Him and magnify His Name.*

> *And He will make a way of salvation and deliverance for you!*

QUESTIONS FOR REVIEW

1. What is the difference between praising God and offering the sacrifice of praise?

2. What happened when King Jehoshaphat went to war and put the praisers in front of the army?

3. How is what happened to King Jehoshaphat an example for us today?

Lesson Eleven

Our Priestly Function of Praise

Introduction

The primary ministry of the early church was ministering to the Lord.

Acts 13:1-3 Now in the church that was at Antioch there were certain prophets and teachers ... As they ministered to the Lord and fasted, the Holy Spirit said, "Now separate to Me Barnabas and Saul for the work to which I have called them." Then, having fasted and prayed, and laid hands on them, they sent them away.

When the church began to let this primary ministry slip away, other ministries became more and more necessary. The church needed ministry to the sick, to those tormented by demon spirits, to the poor, and to the desolate. Counseling ministries began to deal with emotional problems, marriage problems, those addicted to alcohol and drugs, youth in rebellion, and abused children. The list goes on and on. Divorce, adultery, fornication and sexual perversion began to invade the church.

Could it be, when the body of Christ returns to its original ministry of praise and worship, all these other ministries will become less and less necessary? Many times when a group enters into true praise and worship, many begin to be healed emotionally, physically, and even receive deliverance as they come into the presence of God.

Ministering as Priests

Even as Jesus is our High Priest, we share in His priesthood. Every believer is a priest unto God.

Revelation 1:6 And has made us kings and priests to His God and Father, to Him be glory and dominion forever and ever.

Our royal priesthood is revealed in type by Melchizedek. It is later revealed by the priestly ministry of King David. Both of these priesthoods were fulfilled in the priestly ministry of Jesus. Jesus is the eternal High Priest and we are to operate as believer-priests under, or through, Him.

It is necessary to study the functions of the Old Testament Priesthood so that we may receive a clear revelation of our functions as priests as we offer our continual sacrifice of praise.

A ROYAL PRIESTHOOD

Melchizedek

Genesis 14:18 Then Melchizedek king of Salem brought out bread and wine; he was the priest of God Most High.

Melchizedek was the King-Priest of Salem (present day location of Jerusalem). Abraham offered tithes to this one whose name meant "king of righteousness." In contrast to the Aaronic Priesthood, Melchizedek had no recorded genealogy. He was a High Priest chosen by God, not one appointed by the law.

In Psalms, we find a prophetic reference to Jesus being a Priest after the order of Melchizedek.

Psalm 110:4 The LORD has sworn And will not relent, "You are a priest forever According to the order of Melchizedek."

The writer of the book of Hebrews reveals the Priestly ministry of Jesus as a royal King-Priest who would remain a priest forever in the order of Melchizedek.

Hebrews 7:1-3,17 For this Melchizedek, king of Salem, priest of the Most High God, who met Abraham returning from the slaughter of the kings and blessed him, to whom also Abraham gave a tenth part of all, first being translated "king of righteousness," and then also king of Salem, meaning "king of peace," without father, without mother, without genealogy, having neither beginning of days nor end of life, but made like the Son of God, remains a priest continually.

For He testifies: "You are a priest forever according to the order of Melchizedek."

The function of the Melchizedek Priesthood was to "draw near to God." The word, priest, means "to draw near."

Hebrews 7:19 For the law made nothing perfect; on the other hand, there is the bringing in of a better hope, through which we draw near to God.

David: King/Priest

David, as King, also functioned as Priest. He set up the Tabernacle of David, brought back the Ark, and established the sacrifice of praise. As David functioned in his Melchizedek style of priesthood, he typified the coming priestly ministry of Jesus. As David led the people in praise and worship, he was leading them into drawing near to God.

Fulfilled in Jesus

Because of the priestly ministry of Jesus, we as priests can enter boldly into the Presence of God and draw near to Him in our praise and worship.

A HOLY PRIESTHOOD – AARON

Aaron was appointed the first High Priest and his sons were appointed priests. Their sons would also be priests. The Aaronic Priesthood was decided by genealogy.

Leviticus 21:17,21   Speak to Aaron, saying: 'No man of your descendants in succeeding generations, who has any defect, may approach to offer the bread of his God.

Perfection Required

No man of the descendants of Aaron the priest, who has a defect, shall come near to offer the offerings made by fire to the LORD. He has a defect; he shall not come near to offer the bread of his God.'

As the priests were making an offering, they were an earthly picture, or type, of Jesus. Jesus was perfect, and was always pictured as perfect, so no one with a defect could fulfill that picture.

Today, believers are made perfect in Him.

Clothing

The clothing of the priests was distinctive from all other men, even when they were not ministering. God gave definite instructions as to what they were to wear at all times. Each piece of garment was a type of our relationship with God.

The garments when ministering consisted of four parts:

- *Linen breeches*
- *Coat of one piece, without a seam*
- *Four-colored girdle*
- *Linen head covering*

Linen always represents righteousness and we are the righteousness of God.

2 Corinthians 5:21   For He made Him who knew no sin to be sin for us, that we might become the righteousness of God in Him.

They could not wear wool because wool causes one to perspire. Perspiration is a symbol of the curse and of self-effort. Wool can never be thoroughly cleaned.

Anointing

Then, priests anointed with oil – a symbol of the Holy Spirit.

Today, believer-priests have the Holy Spirit abiding within them.

DESCRIPTION OF PRIESTLY FUNCTIONS

Keep Fires Burning

The priests were to keep the fire burning on the altar of sacrifice.

Leviticus 6:9,13 Command Aaron and his sons, saying, 'This is the law of the burnt offering: the burnt offering shall be on the hearth upon the altar all night until morning, and the fire of the altar shall be kept burning on it.

A perpetual fire shall burn on the altar; it shall never go out.'

Paul instructed Timothy to fan up the fire within him.

2 Timothy 1:6 Therefore I remind you to stir up the gift of God which is in you through the laying on of my hands.

In the parable of the ten virgins, Jesus warned us of the necessity of keeping the fire burning in our own lives.

Clear Out Ashes

The priests were to clear the ashes from the altar.

Leviticus 6:10,11 And the priest shall put on his linen garment, and his linen trousers he shall put on his body, and take up the ashes of the burnt offering which the fire has consumed on the altar, and he shall put them beside the altar. Then he shall take off his garments, put on other garments, and carry the ashes outside the camp to a clean place.

A fire cannot continue to burn if the ashes are allowed to accumulate. We can become so enamored in the bright, comfortable "fires" of yesterday that we do not go on to what the Spirit is saying today. We can be smothered by memories of the past. We must be willing to leave the past, both good and bad experiences, if we are to go on and be in the middle of what God is doing today.

Philippians 3:13 Brethren, I do not count myself to have apprehended; but one thing I do, forgetting those things which are behind and reaching forward to those things which are ahead.

Offer Sacrifices

The priests were the only ones who could offer sacrifices.

Exodus 29:38,39,42 Now this is what you shall offer on the altar: two lambs of the first year, day by day continually. One lamb you

shall offer in the morning, and the other lamb you shall offer at twilight.

This shall be a continual burnt offering throughout your generations at the door of the tabernacle of meeting before the LORD, where I will meet you to speak with you.

We are commanded to offer sacrifices of praise.

Give Blessing

The priests were to bless the people.

Leviticus 9:22 Then Aaron lifted his hand toward the people, blessed them, and came down from offering the sin offering, the burnt offering, and peace offerings.

Numbers 6:23-27 Speak to Aaron and his sons, saying, 'This is the way you shall bless the children of Israel. Say to them: "The LORD bless you and keep you; the LORD make His face shine upon you, and be gracious to you; the LORD lift up His countenance upon you, and give you peace." '

"So they shall put My name on the children of Israel, and I will bless them."

Jesus said that we are the salt of the earth. We are to be a blessing to those around us.

Matthew 5:13a You are the salt of the earth; but if the salt loses its flavor, how shall it be seasoned?

Physical Offerings

The priests always came into the Presence of the Lord with an offering.

1 Chronicles 16:29 Ascribe to the Lord the glory due his name. Bring an offering and come before him; worship the Lord in the splendor of his holiness.

Exodus 23:15 You shall keep the Feast of Unleavened Bread (you shall eat unleavened bread seven days, as I commanded you, at the time appointed in the month of Abib, for in it you came out of Egypt; none shall appear before Me empty).

Exodus 34:20 But the firstling of a donkey you shall redeem with a lamb. And if you will not redeem him, then you shall break his neck. All the firstborn of your sons you shall redeem. And none shall appear before Me empty-handed.

Deuteronomy 16:17 Every man shall give as he is able, according to the blessing of the LORD your God which He has given you.

Sacrificial Offerings

One function of the Aaronic priests was to offer sacrifices. We are still to offer spiritual sacrifices.

1 Peter 2:5 **You also, as living stones, are being built up a spiritual house, a holy priesthood, to offer up spiritual sacrifices acceptable to God through Jesus Christ.**

Hebrews 13:15 **Therefore by Him let us continually offer the sacrifice of praise to God, that is, the fruit of our lips, giving thanks to His name.**

We are to come with praise, worship, adoration and thanksgiving, expressing our praise in songs, rejoicing, and with our substance.

REQUIREMENTS OF AARONIC PRIESTHOOD

It is important to understand four things that pertained to the Old Testament priests.

Set Apart

The position of the priest was to be sanctified, or set apart from the world.

Exodus 19:22 **Also let the priests who come near the LORD sanctify themselves, lest the LORD break out against them.**

Holy

The priests must be holy, completely consecrated unto the Lord.

Numbers 16:5 **And he spoke to Korah and all his company, saying, "Tomorrow morning the LORD will show who is His and who is holy, and will cause him to come near to Him; that one whom He chooses He will cause to come near to Him."**

Ordained

The ministry and function of the priests was to draw near to God. The priest represented the people and the people were to be:

➢ *Separated from others of the world*

➢ *A holy nation, a peculiar people*

➢ *A nation of priests unto God*

Exodus 19:4-6a **You have seen what I did to the Egyptians, and how I bore you on eagles' wings and brought you to Myself. Now therefore, if you will indeed obey My voice and keep My covenant, then you shall be a special treasure to Me above all people; for all the earth is Mine. And you shall be to Me a kingdom of priests and a holy nation.**

Cleansed

Priests were required to wash hands and feet before ministering.

Exodus 30:21 So they shall wash their hands and their feet, lest they die. And it shall be a statute forever to them – to him and his descendants throughout their generations.

Exodus 40:12,13 Then you shall bring Aaron and his sons to the door of the tabernacle of meeting and wash them with water. You shall put the holy garments on Aaron, and anoint him and sanctify him, that he may minister to Me as priest.

➤ *Jacob's Family*

Jacob made sure that all in his house were cleansed before he sought the Lord in his distress.

Genesis 35:2,3 And Jacob said to his household and to all who were with him, "Put away the foreign gods that are among you, purify yourselves, and change your garments. Then let us arise and go up to Bethel; and I will make an altar there to God, who answered me in the day of my distress and has been with me in the way which I have gone."

➤ *The People*

Moses commanded the people of Israel to sanctity themselves and to wash their clothes.

Exodus 19:10 Then the LORD said to Moses, "Go to the people and sanctify them today and tomorrow, and let them wash their clothes."

Today, we as believer-priests must be cleansed from any sin in our lives before coming to offer our praise.

1 John 1:9 If we confess our sins, He is faithful and just to forgive us our sins and to cleanse us from all unrighteousness.

We must spend time daily in the Word. As we read, meditate, and obey God's Word, Christ in His love for us is making us holy.

Ephesians 5:25-27 Husbands, love your wives, just as Christ also loved the church and gave Himself for it, that He might sanctify and cleanse it with the washing of water by the word, that He might present it to Himself a glorious church, not having spot or wrinkle or any such thing, but that it should be holy and without blemish.

A WARNING

Nadab and Abihu were sons of Aaron, properly ordained priests, but they entered the Presence of God improperly.

Leviticus 10:1-3 Then Nadab and Abihu, the sons of Aaron, each took his censer and put fire in it, put incense on it, and offered profane fire before the LORD, which He had not commanded them. So fire went out from the LORD and devoured them, and they died before the LORD. Then Moses said to Aaron, "This is what the LORD spoke, saying: 'By those who come near Me I must be regarded as holy; and before all the people I must be glorified.' " So Aaron held his peace.

To be a priest was an honor and a privilege that required total obedience.

It is important that we as believer-priests know and obey the instructions of God's Word as we come to offer our praise to Him. We must not come in carelessness, disobedience, or with a desire to do it our own way, or according to our own traditions if they do not measure up to God's pattern and instruction for praise. We must take care that the songs, music and customs of this world or of other religions do not creep into our worship as represented by the "unauthorized fire" that Nadab and Abihu used in offering their sacrifices before the Lord.

1 Peter 2:9 But you are a chosen generation, a royal priesthood, a holy nation, His own special people, that you may proclaim the praises of Him who called you out of darkness into His marvelous light.

QUESTIONS FOR REVIEW

1. According to 1 Peter 2:5 and Hebrews 13:15, what are the sacrifices that we as believer-priests offer unto the Lord.

2. The priests of the Old Testament had to be cleansed before ministering unto the Lord with their sacrifices. According to 1 John 1:9 and Ephesians 5:25-27, how are we to be cleansed before coming to God with our praise?

3. What lessons can we learn from the experiences of Nadab and Abihu?

Lesson Twelve

Living as Priests

As believer-priests who minister unto the Lord in praise and worship, we must know our calling, our walk, our clothing, and our offerings.

1 Peter 2:5,9 You also, as living stones, are being built up a spiritual house, a holy priesthood, to offer up spiritual sacrifices acceptable to God through Jesus Christ.

But you are a chosen generation, a royal priesthood, a holy nation, His own special people, that you may proclaim the praises of Him who called you out of darkness into His marvelous light.

CHOSEN FOR PRIESTHOOD

Jesus is now our High Priest.

Hebrews 7:15-17 And it is yet far more evident if, in the likeness of Melchizedek, there arises another priest Who has come, not according to the law of a fleshly commandment, but according to the power of an endless life. For He testifies: "You are a priest forever according to the order of Melchizedek."

Hebrews 8:1 Now this is the main point of the things we are saying: We have such a High Priest, who is seated at the right hand of the throne of the Majesty in the heavens.

A Kingdom of Priests

God's desire for the children of Israel was that they would be a kingdom of priests.

Exodus 19:6a And you shall be to Me a kingdom of priests and a holy nation.

God's desire has not changed. Every believer is a priest. Since we are "in Christ," we share his priesthood.

Revelation 1:6 And has made us kings and priests to His God and Father, to Him be glory and dominion forever and ever. Amen.

WALKING WORTHY OF OUR CALLING

Paul urged us to live a life worthy of our calling.

Ephesians 4:1 I, therefore, the prisoner of the Lord, beseech you to have a walk worthy of the calling with which you were called.

A Holy People

Hebrews 12:14 Pursue peace with all men, and holiness, without which no one will see the Lord.

1 Peter 1:15,16 But as He who called you is holy, you also be holy in all your conduct, because it is written, "Be holy, for I am holy."

Ephesians 5:27 That He might present it to Himself a glorious church, not having spot or wrinkle or any such thing, but that it should be holy and without blemish.

A Clean Conscience

The requirements for worship have not changed. Just as God required certain things of the priests, He requires them of us.

Hebrews 10:22 Let us draw near with a true heart in full assurance of faith, having our hearts sprinkled from an evil conscience and our bodies washed with pure water.

Through the blood of Jesus, we can enter His Presence with confidence.

A United Heart

Psalm 86:11 Teach me Your way, O LORD; I will walk in Your truth; unite my heart to fear Your name.

"Unite my heart to fear Your name" means to bring every thought into a unity of worship. It is an insult to God to seem to worship Him, but in reality have our mind on other things!

James 4:8,10 Draw near to God and He will draw near to you. Cleanse your hands, you sinners; and purify your hearts, you double-minded.

Humble yourselves in the sight of the Lord, and He will lift you up.

A Pure Heart

Psalms 24:3,4 Who may ascend into the hill of the LORD? Or who may stand in His holy place? He who has clean hands and a pure heart, who has not lifted up his soul to an idol, nor sworn deceitfully.

Clean hands and a pure heart indicates our motives.

Are we entering into worship to be seen of others?

Are we worshiping to gain God's approval and thus an answer to something we want?

We should examine our motives before God.

A Broken Spirit

Psalm 51:17 The sacrifices of God are a broken spirit, a broken and a contrite heart-These, O God, You will not despise.

A broken spirit is one that has learned discipline and obedience. One that is yielded to the Lordship of Jesus.

Reverent Towards God

Psalm 89:7 God is greatly to be feared in the assembly of the saints, and to be held in reverence by all those who are around Him.

Separated from World

Colossians 1:13 He has delivered us from the power of darkness and translated us into the kingdom of the Son of His love.

OUR PRIESTLY CLOTHING

Clothed with Salvation

Hebrews 12:14 Pursue peace with all men, and holiness, without which no one will see the Lord.

> *Garment of Praise*

Isaiah 61:3 To console those who mourn in Zion, to give them beauty for ashes, the oil of joy for mourning, the garment of praise for the spirit of heaviness; that they may be called trees of righteousness, the planting of the LORD, that He may be glorified.

It is important that we put on our garments of praise. Great importance is given in the scriptures to the importance of the garments of the Old Testament priests. We are believer-priests in spirit and our clothing is of the spirit.

> *Linens of Righteousness*

Revelation 7:9 After these things I looked, and behold, a great multitude which no one could number, of all nations, tribes, peoples, and tongues, standing before the throne and before the Lamb, clothed with white robes, with palm branches in their hands.

Revelation 19:8 And to her it was granted to be arrayed in fine linen, clean and bright, for the fine linen is the righteous acts of the saints.

OUR PRIESTLY OFFERING

Thanksgiving/Praise

Much of the purpose and functions of the Old Testament priests were in the offerings they made to God. Today, we have distinct and definite offerings that we are to make to God.

We are to enter His Presence with praise.

Psalm 100:4 Enter into His gates with thanksgiving, and into His courts with praise. Be thankful to Him, and bless His name.

Our Possessions

We are to enter His Presence with offerings.

Proverbs 3:9,10 Honor the LORD with your possessions, and with the firstfruits of all your increase; so your barns will be filled with plenty, and your vats will over flow with new wine.

Ourselves

We are to bring ourselves as an offering.

Romans 12:1 I beseech you therefore, brethren, by the mercies of God, that you present your bodies a living sacrifice, holy, acceptable to God, which is your reasonable service.

1 Thessalonians 5:23 Now may the God of peace Himself sanctify you completely; and may your whole spirit, soul, and body be preserved blameless at the coming of our Lord Jesus Christ.

Sacrifice of Praise

Hebrews 13:15,16 Therefore by Him let us continually offer the sacrifice of praise to God, that is, the fruit of our lips, giving thanks to His name. But do not forget to do good and to share, for with such sacrifices God is well pleased.

The word, "sacrifice" implies that praise is not always easy, or convenient. And yet, it is to be offered continually.

LIVE AS PRIESTS OR HOLD TRADITIONS

Everyday we are faced with a decision. Do we live as priests, or do we hold on to our traditions, our usual way of doing things?

1 Peter 2:5 You also, as living stones, are being built up a spiritual house, a holy priesthood, to offer up spiritual sacrifices acceptable to God through Jesus Christ.

Enter as Priests Entered

The Aaronic priest entered daily into the Tabernacle of Moses and later into Solomon's Temple. Today we also are to come daily into His Presence.

The Tabernacle of Moses had gates which led into the courts. The priests entered this way to "minister to the Lord" in the Holy Place. Once a year, the High Priest entered into the Holy of Holies which contained the Ark of the Covenant.

The Holy of Holies was the earthly parallel of the heavenly throne room of God. The Ark of the Covenant, which was covered with the Mercy Seat was a type of the throne of God. To be in the Holy of Holies was to be in the very Presence of God.

When Jesus died on the cross, the physical veil which separated the Holy Place from the Holy of Holies was supernaturally torn from top to bottom. Mankind was no longer separated from God. Now through the blood of Jesus, every believer could enter boldly into God's Presence.

Even as there was a progression of "entering in" by the Old Testament priests, there is a progression as we come daily into the Presence of God. We are to "enter in" daily in our own private time of praise and worship. We are also to enter in corporately when we assemble together.

➤ *Through Gates*

Psalm 100:4 Enter into His gates with thanksgiving ...

To "enter" requires an act of obedience. We are to come with thanksgiving – not with ungrateful hearts. Our first songs should be ones that express our heart-felt thanksgiving to the Lord. As we begin to thank and then praise Him, we are moving from the natural circumstances around us into the spirit realm.

➤ *Courtyard*

... And into His courts with praise.

As we pass through the gates, we are in the courtyard. We are not ready to rush into the Holy of Holies of His Presence, into the most intimate time of awesome worship, until we have first spent time in the courtyard of praise. In the court, we are instructed to praise. We joyfully enter with music, singing, clapping and raising our hands unto the Lord, oftentimes dancing before the Lord as we express our praise to Him.

➤ *Holy Place*

Be thankful to Him, and bless His name.

As we linger in the courts of praise, we feel a drawing to come closer, into the Presence of God. We are overcome by thoughts of who He is. We enter a higher form of praise. We find ourselves in the inner court, in the Holy Place.

We are no longer dancing or clapping our hands. We are at that moment so aware of the Presence of God that our hands begin to raise to Him in awesome reverence. The tempo has slowed or even stopped. What was "in order" a moment before has changed. The holiness of God's Presence is almost overwhelming.

> *Holy of Holies*

At times, tears will flow down our cheeks. Sometimes, all that we can do is to stop the music and singing and remain silent before His Holy Presence. We are unaware of those around us. We are totally aware of God. We are standing, kneeling, sometimes even prostrate in His Presence, lost in His Love.

Without realizing it, we have passed, even as the High Priest of old, from the Holy Place into the Holy of Holies.

We have an example of the awesomeness of God when the Ark of the Covenant was brought into Solomon's Temple,

1 Kings 8:10,11 And it came to pass, when the priests came out of the holy place, that the cloud filled the house of the LORD, so that the priests could not continue ministering because of the cloud; for the glory of the LORD filled the house of the LORD.

Or Cling to Traditions

Many who, in the church of their tradition, have sung softly and somberly from a hymnbook, feel awkward in being demonstrative in their praise. Many feel it is not "fitting" to be demonstrative in their praise to God. David wrote,

Psalms 33:1 (NIV) Sing Joyfully to the Lord, you righteous; it is fitting for the upright to praise him.

Psalm 147:1 (NIV) Praise the Lord. How good it is to sing praises to our God, how pleasant and fitting for the upright to praise him!

We must choose to obey God. We must step out of the comfort zone of our traditions and enter fully and whole-heartedly into the biblical expressions of praise to receive all God has for us.

God has a reason for instructing us to rejoice, to clap our hands, to shout, and even to dance. Our praise is fulfilling to Him, and we need to give it. The benefits are ours!

QUESTIONS FOR REVIEW

1. Old Testament priests were clothed with certain garments. Describe the "clothing" of the New Testament priesthood.

2. What are the offerings we are to give to God?

3. Describe the progression of entering into God's Presence that we are to experience in praise and worship.

Victory Through Praise and Worship

WORSHIP IN SPIRIT

Jesus said,

John 4:24 God is Spirit, and those who worship Him must worship in spirit and truth.

We can praise God with our whole heart, soul and body. But we can only worship Him in the spirit.

Like the High Priest on the Day of Atonement, we have moved within the veil. This is an awesome moment. If the High Priest had sin in his life, he knew that he would die in God's Holy Presence. Things that we have been getting by with in the courtyard, will no longer be allowed in our lives. It would be as the day that Ananias and Sapphira lied to the Holy Spirit in Acts five.

To worship in truth means "as not concealing." We stand transparent, open before Him, with nothing concealed. Like the High Priest of old, we must have prepared ourselves to come into His Presence. All sin must be forgiven and cleansed by the blood of Jesus.

1 John 1:9 If we confess our sins, He is faithful and just to forgive us our sins and to cleanse us from all unrighteousness.

Translated Within the Veil

On the Day of Atonement, the High Priest stood in the Holy Place ready to go within the veil. He had the hyssop in one hand and the basin of blood in the other. The veil stretched from wall to wall and from floor to ceiling. There was no way to crawl under, over, or around. There was no door.

The writer of the book of Hebrews referred to this when he wrote,

Hebrews 9:8 The Holy Spirit indicating this, that the way into the Holiest of All was not yet made manifest while the first tabernacle was still standing.

When the priest entered within the veil, he entered totally in the realm of the spirit. He was coming to worship "in spirit and in truth." Could it be, the High Priest was translated in the spirit within the veil just as Philip was translated by the Spirit from the waters where he had just baptized the Ethiopian eunuch to the distant city of Azotus?

To enter into true worship, we must be moved into the realm of the Spirit. God is Spirit, and Jesus said that those who worship Him must worship in the spirit.

Linger in His Presence

As we enter His Presence, our hearts are saying with David, "I want to seek His face." How often have we been seeking God's hand, desiring that our fleshly desires be fulfilled.

Many times, we have come into His overwhelming presence during times of corporate worship. Feeling this awesome anointing of God, someone has felt this was a signal to perform, and has turned back to the "outer court" to give an utterance in tongues, interpretation, or prophecy. Soon, the strong anointing has left and the people are asked to be seated and we have gone "on with the program."

Our heavenly Father is left standing alone. How He had longed for us to come and spend time with Him.

We need to learn to linger in His Presence.

Be Conformed to His Image

In the courtyard, while we are dancing before the Lord with all our might, a breakthrough comes in the spirit. The shells of religious tradition and spiritual indifference fall off. The soil of our heart, like clay in the potter's hands, is softened and warmed toward God.

During times of prolonged and intimate worship as He holds us close to Himself, like soft clay pressed into a mold, we are conformed to His image.

Romans 8:29 For whom He foreknew, He also predestined to be conformed to the image of His Son ...

2 Corinthians 3:18 But we all, with unveiled face, beholding as in a mirror the glory of the Lord, are being transformed into the same image from glory to glory, just as by the Spirit of the Lord.

BUILD ALTARS OF WORSHIP

Over and over throughout the Old Testament, individuals or groups, built altars of praise for what God had done. The Hebrew word for altar means "place of sacrifice."

God is still speaking to His people about building spiritual altars. We do this by coming to Him alone, or in groups, making sacrifice through praise and worship.

Abraham – Mount Moriah

As we studied in Lesson One, the first time the word "worship" was used is when Abraham was going to build an altar on Mount Moriah in obedience to God's command to sacrifice his son, Isaac.

Genesis 22:5 And Abraham said to his young men, "Stay here with the donkey; the lad and I will go yonder and worship, and we will come back to you."

From this "first mention" of worship, we learn that worship is an act of obedience which demands intense sacrifice!

Because of Abraham's obedience in worship, God provided a substitute sacrifice for Isaac. He revealed Himself as Jehovah-Jireh – The Lord, Our Provider.

Genesis 22:13,14a Then Abraham lifted his eyes and looked, and there behind him was a ram caught in a thicket by its horns. So Abraham went and took the ram, and offered it up for a burnt offering instead of his son. And Abraham called the name of the place, The-Lord-Will-Provide.

➤ *Why Mount Moriah?*

Why did God send Abraham to the land of Moriah and when there to a certain mountain? Why was where Abraham made the sacrifice so important? Why did God refer to his only son?

Genesis 22:2 And He said, "Take now your son, your only son Isaac, whom you love, and go to the land of Moriah, and offer him there as a burnt offering on one of the mountains of which I shall tell you."

Many believe that Mount Moriah, where Abraham was obedient and willing to offer His son was the place where Jesus, God's only Son, was crucified. It was there God provided the atoning, substitute sacrifice for our sins.

Were the years Abraham waited for the prophecy to be fulfilled, the years that it took for him to be perfected in faith and obedience so that he could come to this very place?

Visitations Follow Worship

Everywhere Abraham, Isaac and Jacob went, they built altars of worship to God.

Many times the Scriptures reveal that following the building of an altar, there was an appearance of angels, or an appearance of God Himself, at the place where the altar was built.

When we worship God in spirit and in truth, we are building spiritual altars.

Abraham/Isaac – Bethel

In Genesis twelve, we are told that Abraham built an altar at Bethel. Years later Jacob came to Bethel and He had a dream of what was happening there in the realm of the spirit.

Genesis 28:12,13a Then he dreamed, and behold, a ladder was set up on the earth, and its top reached to heaven; and there the angels of God were ascending and descending on it. And behold, the LORD stood above it and said ...

God appeared and spoke to Isaac at Bethel. Awesome things happen in the spirit realm in places where we have had breakthroughs in praise and worship.

Worship Opens the Gate

Genesis 28:16,17 Then Jacob awoke from his sleep and said, "Surely the LORD is in this place, and I did not know it." And he was afraid and said, "How awesome is this place! This is none other than the house of God, and this is the gate of heaven!"

Through worship, the gate of heaven had been opened.

Psalm 24:7 Lift up your heads, O you gates! And be lifted up, you everlasting doors! And the King of glory shall come in.

David – Shepherd's Fields

Was it just a coincidence that David when he was a shepherd, spent hours and hours praising God in the fields outside Bethlehem? Or did he open the gate of heaven, as he worshiped God?

It was here, hundreds of years later at the time of Jesus' birth, the angels appeared to the shepherds and sang,

Luke 2:14 Glory to God in the highest, and on earth peace, good will toward men.

PRAISE OPENS THE VEIL

The Veil of Darkness

Lucifer was the anointed cherub that covers. His nature is to cover. But now, instead of covering the throne of heaven with glorious praise and worship, he covers the earth with a veil of darkness.

Isaiah 60:2 For behold, the darkness shall cover the earth, and deep darkness the people; but the LORD will arise over you, and His glory will be seen upon you.

Satan has assigned prince rulers of darkness over territories.

Ephesians 6:12 For we do not wrestle against flesh and blood, but against principalities, against powers, against the rulers of the darkness of this age, against spiritual hosts of wickedness in the heavenly places.

The purpose of the veil of darkness is to blind all humanity, to keep them from receiving God's glory.

2 Corinthians 4:3,4 But even if our gospel is veiled, it is veiled to those who are perishing, whose minds the god of this age has blinded, who do not believe, lest the light of the gospel of the glory of Christ, who is the image of God, should shine on them.

Powerful Warfare

Powerful things happen when we establish altars of praise and worship. The "surface of the covering" of the veil of spiritual darkness is torn apart and destroyed. The ruler of darkness over that territory is defeated.

Isaiah 25:7 And He will destroy on this mountain the surface of the covering cast over all people, and the veil that is spread over all nations.

When we open up the heavens through praise and worship: the angels can appear; God Himself can come; and His Presence can be felt.

Example of Daniel

In Daniel chapter ten, the angel that was dispatched in response to Daniel's words, was withstood for twenty-one days by the prince of the kingdom of Persia.

Spiritual warfare took place in the heavens. The angel was delayed by the ruler of darkness over the kingdom of Persia until the Archangel Michael came to help him. In response to Daniel's words, the veil of darkness was opened and the angel broke through.

JEHOSHAPHAT'S VICTORY

The victory of Jehoshaphat is one of the greatest examples of winning through praise and worship. We studied about this in more detail in Lesson Ten.

When Judah was being invaded by the armies of three nations, they found themselves hopelessly outnumbered. But King Jehoshaphat and the people of Judah knew what to do. They sought the Lord.

2 Chronicles 20:15 The Spirit of the Lord came upon Jahaziel and he spoke the word of the Lord, do not be afraid nor dismayed because of this great multitude, for the battle is not yours, but God's.

Position Yourselves!

vs.17a,18 You will not need to fight in this battle. Position yourselves, stand still and see the salvation of the LORD, who is with you. And Jehosphaphat bowed his head with his face to the ground, and all Judah and the inhabitants of Jerusalem bowed before the LORD, worshiping the LORD.

The word of the Lord came for them to "position themselves" and they did though worship!

v.19 Then the Levites of the children of the Kohathites and of the children of the Korahites stood up to praise the LORD God of Israel with voices loud and high.

Put Praisers in Front

vs.21,22 And when he had consulted with the people, he appointed those who should sing to the LORD, and who should praise the beauty of holiness, as they went out before the army and were saying: "Praise the LORD, for His mercy endures forever."

Now when they began to sing and to praise, the LORD set ambushes against the people of Ammon, Moab, and Mount Seir, who had come against Judah; and they were defeated .

Enemy Destroyed One Another

vs.23,24 For the people of Ammon and Moab stood up against the inhabitants of Mount Seir to utterly kill and destroy them. And when they had made an end of the inhabitants of Seir, they helped to destroy one another. So when Judah came to a place overlooking the wilderness, they looked toward the multitude; and there were their dead bodies, fallen on the earth. No one had escaped.

Even when it appears that the enemy has us outnumbered and surrounded, if we position ourselves in the Lord, and begin to praise and worship Him, a breakthrough comes in the spirit realm.

God inhabits the praises of His saints.

WARFARE THROUGH PRAISE

Our enemies, who once were the praisers in heaven, cannot stand the sound of praise. Dispatched by the Lord, the warrior angels will ambush the evil forces. In confusion, they will turn on one another and they will be defeated when we begin to praise the Lord.

Many, when they learn that we are at war with the enemy, spend a lot of their time screaming at the devil and his demons. They focus on the enemy.

There is a place for warfare music today. It should remind us of our victorious authority over the enemy, and remind him he has already been defeated!

Victorious warfare is not screaming at the enemy. It is praise centered. It is focused on the greatness of our God.

Psalm 149:6-9 Let the high praises of God be in their mouth, and a two-edged sword in their hand, to execute vengeance on the nations, and punishments on the peoples; to bind their kings with chains, and their nobles with fetters of iron; to execute on them the written judgment–this honor have all His saints. Praise the LORD!

Isaiah 30:32 And in every place where the staff of punishment passes, which the LORD lays on him, it will be with tambourines and harps; and in battles of brandishing He will fight with it.

The praisers in front of Jehoshaphat's army were not singing warfare songs directed at the devil. They were singing, **Praise the beauty of holiness. Praise the LORD, for His mercy endures forever.** They were worshiping God!

Paul and Silas

Paul and Silas were stripped, beaten, and thrown into prison with their feet locked in the stocks.

Acts 16:25,26 But at midnight Paul and Silas were praying and singing hymns to God, and the prisoners were listening to them.

Suddenly there was a great earthquake, so that the foundations of the prison were shaken; and immediately all the doors were opened and everyone's chains were loosed.

We must continue to offer the sacrifice of praise, no matter how impossible the situation appears. When we do this, there are always powerful results. Victory can come through high praise and intimate worship. We can agree with David when he wrote,

Psalms 68:1a Let God arise, Let His enemies be scattered ...

QUESTIONS FOR REVIEW

1. How are we to "enter" God's presence in worship?

2. Describe the "breakthrough" that takes place as we worship God.

3. How did the armies of Judah under King Jehosaphat receive their breakthrough against the surrounding enemies?

Lesson Fourteen

Praise and Worship Leadership

We must follow God's ordained plan and pattern for spiritual leadership in the church if we expect God's anointing upon the praise and worship service.

PASTOR AND OTHER MINISTERING ELDERS

Spiritual Leadership

The pastor and other ministering elders of the church must provide the spiritual leadership, authority, direction and pattern for an effective praise and worship ministry in the church.

1 Peter 5:2,3 Shepherd the flock of God which is among you, serving as overseers, not by constraint but willingly, not for dishonest gain but eagerly; nor as being lords over those entrusted to you, but being examples to the flock.

Active Participation

It is good when the pastor and other ministering elders actively participate in all of the praise and worship from the moment that the service begins. By so doing, they become an example and encourage the congregation to fully participate.

1 Timothy 4:12 Let no one despise your youth, but be an example to the believers in word, in conduct, in love, in spirit, in faith, in purity.

A Good Example

If the ministers come in late, by their actions they seem to place little value upon the time of praise and worship in the church service, and many in the congregation will assume the same attitude.

1 Corinthians 11:1 Imitate me, just as I also imitate Christ.

Preparation for Ministry

The pastor and other ministers also need this time to properly prepare their hearts for the anointing to be released for effective ministry to the people.

Acts 6:2 Then the twelve summoned the multitude of the disciples and said, "It is not desirable that we should leave the word of God and serve tables."

Discerning Flow of Spirit

It is also important for those in the five-fold ministry to avoid other distractions and give themselves completely to discerning the flow and moving of the Holy Spirit for that particular service.

Appointing Worship Leaders

The musicians and worship leaders are to be appointed by the ministering elders of the church and will be ministering under their authority. Possibly the praise and worship will be led by the pastor, one of the prophets or another one of the ministering elders who are gifted in this area.

A biblical example of this is found where King David appointed some of the Levites as musicians to minister before the Lord.

1 Chronicles 16:4 And he appointed some of the Levites to minister before the ark of the LORD, to commemorate, to thank, and to praise the LORD God of Israel.

WORSHIP TEAM APPOINTED BY DAVID

There was a ministry team appointed by David.

Worship Leader

Leadership authority was given to Asaph as the chief musician.

1 Chronicles 16:5 Asaph the chief, and next to him Zechariah, then Jeiel, Shemiramoth, Jehiel, Mattithiah, Eliab, Benaiah, and Obed-Edom: Jeiel with stringed instruments and harps, but Asaph made music with cymbals ...

Choir Leader

A choir leader was also appointed.

1 Chronicles 15:22 Chenaniah, leader of the Levites, was instructor in charge of the music, because he was skillful.

1 Chronicles 15:27b David was clothed with a robe of fine linen, as were all the Levites who bore the ark, the singers, and Chenaniah the music master with the singers.

Instrumentalists

Instrumentalists were also appointed for service.

1 Chronicles 25:6,7 All these were under the direction of their father for the music in the house of the LORD, with cymbals, stringed instruments, and harps, for the service of the house of God. Asaph, Jeduthun, and Heman were under the authority of the king. So the number of them, with their brethren who were instructed in the songs of the LORD, all who were skillful, was two hundred and eighty-eight.

WORSHIP LEADERS – THEIR MINISTRY GIFTINGS AND TRAINING

Functioning as Prophets

Often those whom God has chosen as the worship leaders will have the ministry "gifting" of a prophet. Music is often used to release the Spirit of prophecy into action.

1 Chronicles 25:1a Moreover David and the captains of the army separated for the service some of the sons of Asaph, of Heman, and of Jeduthun, who should prophesy with harps, stringed instruments, and cymbals.

1 Chronicles 25:3 Of Jeduthun, the sons of Jeduthun: Gedaliah, Zeri, Jeshaiah, Shimei, Hashabiah, and Mattithiah, six, under the direction of their father Jeduthun, who prophesied with a harp to give thanks and to praise the LORD.

Trained and Skilled in Music

The calling and responsibility of ministering unto the Lord in music should never be taken lightly. Those who lead in the praise, whether vocalists or instrumentalists, should have intensive training and practice to become skilled musicians.

1 Chronicles 25:6,7 All these were under the direction of their father for the music in the house of the LORD, with cymbals, stringed instruments, and harps, for the service of the house of God. Asaph, Jeduthun, and Heman were under the authority of the king. So the number of them, with their brethren who were instructed in the songs of the LORD, all who were skillful, was two hundred and eighty-eight.

Qualifications of Worship Leaders

➢ *Anointed of God*

One who leads praise and worship must be anointed by God for this special and important ministry in the church. It is a gift and calling from the Holy Spirit that must be respected and cultivated.

1 John 2:20,27 But you have an anointing from the Holy One, and you know all things.

But the anointing which you have received from Him abides in you, and you do not need that anyone teach you; but as the same anointing teaches you concerning all things, and is true, and is not a lie, and just as it has taught you, you will abide in Him.

➢ *A Worshiper*

The praise leaders cannot lead people where they have not been living themselves. Intense praise and worship must be a daily part of the leader's personal life and devotion.

John 4:23,24 But the hour is coming, and now is, when the true worshipers will worship the Father in spirit and truth; for the Father is seeking such to worship Him.

God is Spirit, and those who worship Him must worship in spirit and truth.

➢ *Spiritually Mature*

To be a leader within the body of Christ, a person must be a mature believer. His or her wisdom, experience and skilled spiritual leadership will encourage the total participation of the body.

Ephesians 4:12,13 For the equipping of the saints for the work of ministry, for the edifying of the body of Christ, till we all come to the unity of the faith and the knowledge of the Son of God, to a perfect man, to the measure of the stature of the fullness of Christ.

➢ *Leadership Abilities*

They must be able to motivate and lead people.

1 Corinthians 11:1 Imitate me, just as I also imitate Christ.

➢ *Spiritually Sensitive*

They must be sensitive to follow the anointing and leadership of the Holy Spirit while being alert and sensitive to how the congregation is responding.

Psalm 78:72 So he shepherded them according to the integrity of his heart, and guided them by the skillfulness of his hands.

➢ *In Submission*

They must recognize and submit to the pastor and other spiritual eldership within the church.

1 Peter 5:5 Likewise you younger people, submit yourselves to your elders. Yes, all of you be submissive to one another, and be clothed with humility, for "God resists the proud, but gives grace to the humble."

➢ *Person of Purity, Integrity, Humility*

A worship leader must be a person of proven character, whose personal life and integrity is above reproach. As a humble servant of God, his actions will always call attention to God and never seek to bring glory to himself.

1 Peter 5:6 Therefore humble yourselves under the mighty hand of God, that He may exalt you in due time ...

➤ *Committed and Faithful*

Must be faithful and punctual in the fulfillment of this God-given responsibility.

1 Corinthians 4:2 Moreover it is required in stewards that one be found faithful.

THE INSTRUMENTALIST

Chosen as Skilled Musicians

Often musicians, called by God to play a certain instrument as a part of the worship team, are given supernatural ability to play that instrument. This does not minimize, however, one's responsibility to be trained and to practice faithfully to develop the necessary skill to be counted worthy of one's calling.

1 Chronicles 25:6,7 All these were under the direction of their father for the music in the house of the LORD, with cymbals, stringed instruments, and harps, for the service of the house of God. Asaph, Jeduthun, and Heman were under the authority of the king. So the number of them, with their brethren who were instructed in the songs of the LORD, all who were skillful, was two hundred and eighty-eight.

Instruments

All three types of musical instruments (stringed, wind and percussion) were used in praise and worship.

**Psalms 150:3-5 Praise Him with the sound of the trumpet;
   praise Him with the lute and harp!
Praise Him with the timbrel and dance;
   praise Him with stringed instruments and flutes!
Praise Him with loud cymbals;
   praise Him with high sounding cymbals!**

Even as with the praise and worship as was recorded in the Old Testament, much is added to the dimension and quality of the praise and worship service by using additional instruments as God provides the talent, the instruments and the space for their use.

The leader may choose to add as many instruments as practical while maintaining a proper balance of types of instruments and ratio to the size of the auditorium.

Unity, Harmony, Volume

The instrumentalist must be sensitive and alert to the direction of the leader. Much practice is necessary to be in unity, harmony and balance with the other instruments.

The instruments must support the lyrics by their volume without calling attention to themselves or drowning out the voices of the worshipers.

Sensitive to Spirit

The instrumentalists must be sensitive to the move of the Holy Spirit as "skilled musicians." By so doing, they can release the anointing of God into manifestations of the Spirit during the praise and worship service.

The instrumentalists must be sensitive to flow as one in harmony and unity of sound.

2 Chronicles 34:12 And the men did the work faithfully. Their overseers were Jahath and Obadiah the Levites, of the sons of Merari, and Zechariah and Meshullam, of the sons of the Kohathites, to supervise. Others of the Levites, all of whom were skillful with instruments of music ...

THE CONGREGATION

It is the privilege and responsibility of every believer to enter fully into the praise and worship service.

Hebrews 2:12 Saying: "I will declare Your name to My brethren; in the midst of the congregation I will sing praise to You."

Preparation

Each one must prepare his heart and be in the attitude of praise and worship upon arriving at the church or assembly of believers.

Anticipation

An attitude of anticipation and expectancy should draw us to each praise and worship service.

Punctual

Punctuality shows our respect and love for God. We should not want to miss one moment of the time that we will be spending in His Presence.

As there is a progression of "entering in" from the gates, the courts, the outer and inner courts, we could be left behind and not fully experience true worship unless we take the time to move step by step into His Presence. We should plan to arrive early and prayerfully prepare our spirits and get them quiet and ready to minister unto the Lord in the fullest experience and expression of praise and worship.

Many find great value in a time of prayer prior to the beginning of the praise and worship service.

With Our Whole Hearts

From the first note of the music, we should be in the attitude of joyful anticipation, an intensity of spirit and an expectancy to experience the Presence of God as never before.

We must press in with our spirits and sing and praise God with our whole spirit, soul and body. We should totally lose ourselves in His Presence. Our love for God should be expressed by ministering unto the Lord with all of our energy, our voices, our bodies and our whole hearts.

Psalm 138:1 I will praise You with my whole heart; before the gods I will sing praises to You.

Follow Worship Leader

We should not become so lost in the Spirit that we are not following and flowing with the God-ordained praise and worship leader. We must be sensitive to flow and move with the anointing of the Holy Spirit.

Avoid Distractions

Do not allow yourself to be distracted by your thoughts, or the actions of others.

The song book or words on the overhead projector screen are only to help us to know the words and to sing together. Once these are observed, do not continue to focus your attention on them when it is no longer necessary.

Sometimes it is helpful to close your eyes or look toward the ceiling in order that you may totally forget about all else and concentrate on the Lord. (The worship leaders cannot do this.)

SINGING IN SPIRIT

By following the worship leader and the leadership of the Holy Spirit, there are times when the praise will move into a musical expression of praise in "tongues." At this time, we may become aware that the angels are singing along with us as we sing "in the spirit."

1 Corinthians 14:15 What is the result then? I will pray with the spirit, and I will also pray with the understanding. I will sing with the spirit, and I will also sing with the understanding.

When this happens, release yourself into a free flow in your "heavenly language."

The Holy Spirit will provide not only the words but also the melody as we are sensitive to Him.

Spiritual Song

Be sensitive to the Holy Spirit. Often He desires to give a "spiritual song" to the body. If God wants to minister in this way through you, receive whatever authority that may be required by the leadership before giving it.

It may begin in tongues and then move into your understanding. It may come as prophecy. God will give the words and the melody. New songs of praise are often given to the body of Christ during these times.

Ephesians 5:19 Speaking to one another in psalms and hymns and spiritual songs, singing and making melody in your heart to the Lord ...

Colossians 3:16 Let the word of Christ dwell in you richly in all wisdom, teaching and admonishing one another in psalms and hymns and spiritual songs, singing with grace in your hearts to the Lord.

VOCAL GIFTS OF HOLY SPIRIT

Often there is a pause in the time of praise at the end of a song that gives an opportunity for a message in tongues, interpretation of tongues, or prophecy.

Receive any authority or recognition that may be required by the leadership before giving the message God has given you. It should be given in a way that it can be clearly heard and understood by the whole congregation.

Respect the Silence

Every pause or silence during the time of praise and worship is not necessarily a signal that a message should be given. Be sensitive to the Holy Spirit.

The silence may have come because of the intensity of the Presence of God that we have entered into as we are worshiping Him. To speak at that time would be an interruption of what God wants to happen at that moment.

Habakkuk 2:20 But the LORD is in His holy temple. Let all the earth keep silence before Him.

QUESTIONS FOR REVIEW

1. Describe the biblical qualifications and functions of the worship leaders.

2. Describe the biblical functions of the instrumentalists.

3. What is the congregation's responsibility in praise and worship?

Lesson Fifteen

Ministering as a Worship Leader

PREPARATION

A successful and anointed worship service does not just happen. It takes hours of prayerful preparation before the service begins.

A previous outstanding service will not necessarily be the pattern for what will happen in another. God is a God of variety. Pray and receive His leading for each particular service. Be led of His Spirit and sensitive to His anointing.

Lamentations 3:22,23 Through the Lord's mercies we are not consumed, because His compassions fail not. They are new every morning; great is Your faithfulness.

In some praise and worship services, almost all of the time will be spent in joyful praise toward God. In others, the service will move more quickly into a time of intense worship.

Choosing Songs

When possible, it is important to find out the topic of the message that is planned for the service. Then the songs chosen can flow with, and lay spiritual groundwork for, the teaching of the Word that will follow.

Take time to choose prayerfully the songs that will be used during the praise and worship service.

Choose songs that can be sung in a comfortable voice range for the congregation.

Sometimes repeating songs several times will let the words and message become part of the worshiper's personal thoughts and desires.

Arranging Songs

Arrange the songs in such a way that they will follow the pattern of "entering-in" with songs of thanksgiving; songs of praise that will induce higher and higher levels of physical and vocal participation; songs that will release the anointing of God and the people into soaring levels of praise; and finally songs of worship that will move the believers closer into the Presence of God.

The songs should be grouped in such a way that the worshipers are not moved back and forth between songs of worship and praise, but are progressing in a steady, even flow into higher and higher levels of worship.

Choose carefully the keys in which the songs will be sung and group together certain songs which share a common theme.

It is good to provide the instrumentalists and the overhead projectionist, if one is used, with a list showing the order of the songs and the key in which they will be sung. You may want to provide the instrumentalists with the music, or show where the song is located in a music worship binder. Provide the instrumentalists with the chords to be used for key changes so that the music can continue and flow between songs.

If new songs are to be sung, prepare the overhead transparency if a projector is to be used.

Psalm 33:3 Sing to Him a new song; play skillfully with a shout of joy.

The projectionist should have the transparencies pulled out and arranged in the order that they will be used.

The songs will often flow from one to another without a break so that there can be a steady, even flow of the Spirit.

Spiritual Preparation

A good leader will never come into a service "cold." Preparation includes as much time as it takes in prayer and personal praise and worship to discern the Spirit's theme for the service before the meeting begins. Then he will be able to start the first chorus "on target." Every minute of the service that it takes the leader to move into the flow of the Holy Spirit is time taken from true praise and worship of God.

Physical Preparation

Dress appropriately for the occasion. Do not let your appearance distract the attention of the worshipers.

Personal hygiene, cleanliness and neatness is important as you are representing God before the people.

Genesis 41:14 Then Pharaoh sent and called Joseph, and they brought him hastily out of the dungeon; and he shaved, changed his clothing, and came to Pharaoh.

Leading Worship Team, Vocalist, Instrumentalists

Prayerfully choose each member of the worship team. Maintain spiritual discipline and lovingly, but firmly, deal with any sin or moral issues that may arise.

Demonstrate a high level of spiritual leadership, encouraging and developing the skills of each one. Set high standards of excellence and show appreciation to each one for his or her part. Require faithfulness, commitment and a spirit of unity.

The worship team should pray together prior to the worship service.

PRACTICAL INSTRUCTIONS

Glorify God

Do not draw attention to yourself. The believers are there to see Jesus and to worship Him and the Father.

Matthew 17:8 And when they had lifted up their eyes, they saw no one but Jesus only.

Be Sensitive

It is important that the leader be sensitive to all that is going on during the service.

> ➢ *To God and the leading of His Holy Spirit*
> ➢ *To the co-leaders of the worship service*
> ➢ *To the instrumentalists*
> ➢ *To the wisdom and leadership of the elders*
> ➢ *To the whole congregation*

Be Confident

Be confident in your calling and your ability. In humility, giving God all of the glory, realize that if the Lord has anointed you to lead the worship service, He will give you the ability to do it with excellence.

Philippians 4:13 I can do all things through Christ who strengthens me.

Lead Them In

The people must be led from where they are into the Presence of God. You cannot lead them from where you are, but instead you must skillfully lead them all in, as one body, from the place where they are, into being corporately in the Spirit.

Seek to make immediate contact with the congregation, establish the confidence of the people with your leadership and then quickly move them on into praise.

There are certain songs and spiritual techniques that will serve to draw the people as one body through the "gates" with thanksgiving and in anticipation of experiencing the

Presence of God. The worship leader must develop this ability by the anointing of God as part of his God-ordained skills.

What if They Don't Enter

Quickly discern if the people as a whole are "entering in" and moving as one body into the Presence of the Lord. If not, ask God for His wisdom in how to overcome any hindrances and be able to quickly move ahead.

Exhort them, using care not to bring condemnation, to move into the Presence of God. Lovingly teach them how to enter in. Bind any hindering spirits that may be trying to stop the flow of the Spirit. If necessary move on to another song.

Those Who Will Not

We must realize that there are many reasons why some are not moving with the others into praise and worship. Some may be unbelievers, some may be believers living in rebellion or disobedience to God. Others might be under condemnation from the enemy or under a burden of cares. Some may just not know how.

As a worship leader you must not be distracted by those who will not enter in. How glorious it is when all the people with one heart are all entering in together. However, sometimes we have to ignore those who will not and keep our fullest attention on the corporate body of believers. Sometimes these individuals can be dealt with privately at a later time and instructed, or exhorted, to a greater level of participation.

Keep Eyes Open

When you close your eyes, you are closing out the very people you are to lead into worship. The leader must be aware of what is happening and where the people are spiritually as the praise service is progressing.

The leader must not become so "lost in the Spirit" that he or she loses contact with the people that he or she is leading. The time of being "lost" for the leader is in his or her own worship time or when someone else is leading.

Lead and encourage people by making eye contact with them. Part of the gifting of the worship leader is to enter into true worship while observing the congregation at the same time.

Don't Preach

During praise and worship is not the time to stop and "preach." Short exhortations are sometimes helpful in bringing the people into higher levels of praise. Don't break the flow of the service or use up precious time by speaking about things that will not directly contribute to the moving of the Holy Spirit in praise and worship.

Dealing with Mistakes

Remember that we are all "learners" and making mistakes is part of the learning process. Do not put yourself under condemnation. Be honest with the people if you have missed God and move on in the direction that God is leading.

Sometime after the service is over, spend time alone talking to God about it. Tell Him where you feel that you failed. Ask for insights in being more skillful in handling the same situation the next time it develops.

Above all, let Him speak to you and encourage you about the things that you did right! Let Him lovingly instruct you in the ways of the Spirit. Receive His instruction while rejecting any condemnation from the enemy.

Romans 8:1 There is therefore now no condemnation to those who are in Christ Jesus, who do not walk according to the flesh, but according to the Spirit.

If needed, seek and ask for the council and advice of the pastor or other ministering elders.

THE WORSHIP SERVICE

Exhort People

It is good to exhort the people to sing unto the Lord. They should not sing because it is the custom, or just for enjoyment. They should sing praises unto the Lord and fully enter into His Presence in true worship.

Begin with Thanksgiving

Before we can fully praise God, we must first enter into the place of praise.

Psalm 100:4 Enter into His gates with thanksgiving, and into His courts with praise. Be thankful to Him, and bless His name.

Move on into Praise

Much of the time spent during the praise and worship will be spent here in the "courts." It is here that each one must be released into greater vocal and physical expressions of true praise toward God for all of His wonderful blessings.

Flow on into Worship

Be sensitive to the Holy Spirit as to His timing, and begin to move the people on into true, deep and intimate worship of God for who He is.

Follow Anointing

Be willing to lay aside your plans even if you have spent much time in preparation. You may skip some songs while lingering a longer time upon others.

When a strong anointing of the Holy Spirit begins to come, do not hurry on to the next song. Linger there as long as the anointing is growing in intensity. Continue repeating that song until the Spirit can complete the work that He is doing, bringing the assembly into higher praise, or entering closer into His Presence in worship.

Vocal Gifts

Encourage the spontaneous free flow of the operation of the vocal gifts of the Holy Spirit from among the congregation. Often a pause at the appropriate place will allow time for God to speak to His people through the gifts of tongues and interpretation of tongues or through prophecy.

1 Corinthians 12:7-10 But the manifestation of the Spirit is given to each one for the profit of all: for to one is given the word of wisdom through the Spirit, to another the word of knowledge through the same Spirit, to another faith by the same Spirit, to another gifts of healings by the same Spirit, to another the working of miracles, to another prophecy, to another discerning of spirits, to another different kinds of tongues, to another the interpretation of tongues.

Someone may have a short word of exhortation, a scripture, or a spiritual song.

Psalm 40:3 He has put a new song in my mouth–praise to our God; many will see it and fear, and will trust in the LORD.

The worship leader must retain spiritual authority over the service at all times. In larger assemblies of people, it may be desirable to have a person raise his or her hand or come to one of the elders for recognition before giving a message.

The message may need to be given using the sound system or in a voice loud enough to be heard by the whole congregation.

For Edification

All things should be done for mutual edification. Every scriptural manifestation is legitimate and proper, but everything that is done should be for the edifying of the whole gathering.

1 Corinthians 14:26 How is it then, brethren? Whenever you come together, each of you has a psalm, has a teaching, has a tongue, has a revelation, has an interpretation. Let all things be done for edification.

Avoid Confusion

God is not the author of confusion.

1 Corinthians 14:33a For God is not the author of confusion but of peace ...

If the service begins to move into confusion, take charge and lead it back out of confusion. If necessary, pause and explain what is happening, thus clarifying the situation. Use these times to teach the correct way of moving in the Spirit.

Avoid Intrusions and Cross-Currents

If there is an intrusion in what the flow of the Holy Spirit is doing at that moment, the leader must be mature enough to discern and deal with the situation without further breaking that flow.

Pray and develop the spiritual gift of "distinguishing between spirits." Also learn to be sensitive to God's timing. The intrusion might be a beautiful expression of a vocal gift of the Holy Spirit or a spiritual song that is being given out of God's perfect timing.

The worship leader must have the faith, boldness, discretion, wisdom, grace and tact to skillfully, gently and lovingly lead the service back into the middle of the anointing and flow of the Holy Spirit.

Unity of Spirit

A skillful praise and worship leader will establish a unity between himself and the congregation, between the individuals within the congregation, and among the whole body and the Holy Spirit. While this unity of the Spirit becomes stronger and stronger, true worship will begin to flow in greater and greater measure toward God.

The Time

The worship leader must be alert to stay within the time that has been set by the pastor or elders. If the moving of the Spirit is leading into an extended time of praise and worship, carefully receive the confirmation of that to your spirit and the authority to do so by a signal from the pastor or elder who has the spiritual leadership of the meeting before continuing.

Concluding

Be sensitive to the Holy Spirit in concluding the praise and worship service by gently leaving each worshiper in the Presence of God. Having skillfully led the congregation through the gates with thanksgiving and into the great courtyard experience of praise and then gently moving them into the awesome and intimate Presence of God in true heartfelt worship, you have brought them into His embrace.

Being careful not to disrupt what is happening to the lives and spirits of each believer during that special moment, let each one, as the worship is closing, linger for a moment of silence in the glory of His Presence.

As you walk away, you will know that lives have been changed during that service; that you have skillfully led other believers into experiencing the unspeakable joy of real praise and worship that has brought great pleasure to God Himself.

QUESTIONS FOR REVIEW

1. List some preparations that the skillful worship leader should make prior to the beginning of the praise and worship service.

2. Give one example of how a worship leader can more effectively lead people in greater dimensions of praise and worship.

3. Explain what is meant by "following the anointing" during praise and worship.

Courses in This Series
By A.L. and Joyce Gill

The Authority of the Believer — *How to Quit Losing and Start Winning*

This life-changing study reveals God's provision for mankind's victory and dominion over Satan in the world today. God's eternal purpose for every believer was revealed at creation when God said, "Let them have dominion!" You will be released into a powerful new spirit of boldness as you discover how you can start winning in every struggle of life.

God's Provision for Healing — *Receiving and Ministering God's Healing Power*

This powerful teaching lays a solid Word foundation which releases the faith of the students to receive their own healing, walk in perfect health, and boldly minister healing to others. Many are healed as this revelation comes alive in their spirits.

Supernatural Living — *Through the Gifts of the Holy Spirit*

Every believer can be released into operating in all nine gifts of the Holy Spirit in their daily lives. From an intimate relationship with the Holy Spirit, each person will discover the joy of walking in the supernatural as the vocal, revelation, and power gifts are released.

Patterns for Living — *From the Old Testament*

God never changes! The way He deals with His people has been revealed throughout the Bible. What He did for His people in the Old Testament, He will do for His people today! You can learn the Old Testament truths to help you understand the New Testament.

Praise and Worship — *Becoming Worshipers of God*

Discover the joy of moving into God's presence and releasing your spirit in all of the powerful, fresh, biblical expressions of high praise and intimate worship to God. As you study God's plan for praise and worship, you will become a daily worshiper of God.

The Church Triumphant — *Through the Book of Acts*

Jesus announced, "I will build my Church and the gates of hell will not prevail against it." This thrilling, topical study of the book of Acts reveals that church in action as a pattern for our lives and ministries today. It will inspire us into a new and greater dimension of supernatural living as signs, wonders, and miracles are released in our daily lives.

The Ministry Gifts — *Apostles, Prophets, Evangelists, Pastors, Teachers*

Jesus gave gifts to men! These precious and important gifts are men and women God has called as His Apostles, Prophets, Evangelists, Pastors, and Teachers. Discover how these gifts are being restored to His Church, and how they function to equip the saints for the work of the ministry.

New Creation Image — *Knowing Who You Are in Christ*

This life-changing revelation will free believers from feelings of guilt, condemnation, unworthiness, inferiority and inadequacy, to be conformed to the image of Christ. It will release each believer to enjoy being, doing, and having all for which they were created in God's image.

Miracle Evangelism — *God's Plan to Reach the World* — *By John Ezekiel*

A powerful study which will release believers into becoming daily soul winners in the great end-time harvest through miracle evangelism. Like the believers in the book of Acts, we can experience the joy of reaching the lost as God confirms His Word through signs, wonders, and healing miracles.

**Many of the manuals are available in other languages.
French, Korean, Russian, and Spanish.
There are also teaching tapes and videos that go with most of them.
Call Powerhouse Publishing for more information.
1-800-366-3119**